With love and best wishes Margaret J Price M.B.E

Aiming High

Aiming High

The Story of Margaret Price, MBE

David Hunn

Cartoons by Chic Jacob

Arthur Barker Limited
A subsidiary of Weidenfeld (Publishers) Limited

Published in Great Britain by
Arthur Barker Limited
91 Clapham High Street
London SW4 7TA

ISBN 0 213 16894 4

Contents

Acknowledgements

Tales of this kind don't get written without a lot of help. Apart from the very many hours given to me by Margaret and Frank Price, thanks are due to Margaret's mother, Ivy Hough, to Cliff Last, Senior Technical Officer at Stoke Mandeville, and to those editors and publishers from whose works I have been allowed to quote: *The Observer*, *Archery International*, J.J. Walsh's *Understanding Paraplegia* (published by Tavistock Publications), Sydney Foott's *Handicapped at Home* (Design Council) and *No Grass Between My Toes* by Eve Rimmer and Garth Gilmour (A.H. & A.W. Reed). Above all, I was grateful for the constant presence at my side of Sir Ludwig Guttmann's definitive work on the subject, *Textbook of Sport for the Disabled* (HM + M Publishers, Aylesbury).

I should also like to draw attention to the remarkable contributions made by two *Observer* colleagues: photographer Eamonn McCabe, who took all the track-suited pictures (that on the front cover was voted the sports picture of the year); and cartoonist Chic Jacob, whose work so perfectly reflects the sense of humour with which Margaret Price views life and petty problems like paraplegia.

D.H.

To the memory of a great man: Professor Sir Ludwig Guttmann, CBE, FRS, MD, FRCP, FRCS – affectionately known as 'Poppa' – who showed the disabled how able they are.

'You see things, and say "Why?" But I dream things that never were; and I say "Why not?"'

George Bernard Shaw (*Back to Methuselah*)

1 Jump for joy

Margaret Price was a tomboy before, during and after her schooldays. She would be one now, and remain so to the end, but that it's a bit difficult when you can't kick a ball, climb a tree, slide down banisters, slap a back or swing a cat. Margaret cannot run for shelter, toffee or her life, and though she protests she can stand on her own two feet, she certainly can't stand on anyone else's. She has not been able to stand, walk or even sit unaided for more than ten years, yet during that time she became one of the world's most remarkable athletes.

That would be enough, and more than enough, but it is only the beginning. Somehow, God knows how, she has been able to jump for joy at the dawning of each day. The pitiful slamming of doors along the corridors of her life she has regarded as puny challenges and overcome them, marching through as though they were not there. As her physical potential has diminished, her determination and vivacity have increased, leaving marooned in shame those of us who have been able to sail across our days without noticeable handicap, yet have not the guts to fight against the meanest squall.

She is no saint, that would be too much for the observer to bear. Apart from being more than usually bloody-minded – in her case, a necessary defence – she has her share of defects, and of detractors. But once met, she is hard to forget. Try as one might to behave normally in front of a paraplegic, there is a massive pull on the able-bodied person to be sympathetic and to expect the victim to be pathetic. This is in fact very rarely the case, and certainly has never been with Margaret. When they told her she would never walk again, there were no tears. 'Give us a wheelchair and let's get cracking,' she said. And cracking is what she has got.

Let us look at Margaret Price in her wheelchair. She is likely to be grinning – gap-toothed, big and mischievous, big and delighted, or big and hilarious. You wouldn't know it, but she is more than usually tall, 5ft 8in if you could stretch her out, with wickedly sparkling eyes. Not a beauty, but a honey and a devil; the sort who makes you wonder if the cushion on which you are about to sit down is going to make a rude noise. She is obviously paralysed, though how much is not at first clear. She can extend an arm and shake a hand, if feebly, but there is nothing feeble about her welcome. In two minutes you feel that nothing more tremendous has happened to her for a week than that you should have walked through the door. In half an hour you know that nothing more tremendous has happened to you for years than that you should have walked through the door and found her.

There is something about her that will immediately strike you – and forcibly, if you're not careful. Her right leg sticks straight out in front of her, rigid and immobile, held up on a leg rest. It makes opening doors hellishly difficult, and opening glass ones highly dangerous. She is not too easy to sit opposite at a dinner table, either, and when you wheel her over a pedestrian crossing and round on to the pavement you are liable to mow down a few pedestrians.

Her voice is tinged with the outer London whine, but the substance of her conversation is usually so forceful and her delivery so enthusiastic that stimulation is its regular effect on the listener. She is thirty-four, childless, and married to the man who found her in a guard's van: Frank Price, a bearded Gloucestershire pixie who regards Margaret as his saviour and not himself as hers. There are good reasons for that, but you'll not learn them soon. If you have gone to see them at home, you will know that they live in an old and simple Devon cottage so isolated that bird song rings out like a bugle-call: 'When we first came down here we went out into the garden and I said, "Frank, listen." We listened, and there wasn't a sound.'

Well, that's your introduction to Margaret Price, MBE and proud of it, the woman who has done more than any man alive to demonstrate that disability is no handicap to achievement. By the time meningitis scurrilously crowned her paraplegia in 1981, she was the Disabled Olympic champion in five events and the holder of seven individual world records; but her story is not one of mere sporting glory. If she ever allows her body to be laid to rest, the epitaph might read 'Here lives a triumphant spirit.' And where lives, I wonder, and how lives, the driver who knocked her down on a zebra crossing in Folkestone and was never seen again?

2 Hit and Run

It is a common phenomenon that a person involved in a sudden, severe and traumatic accident retains no memory of the moments immediately preceding the shock; but instead carries a totally incorrect image of the scene, one that is so clear that he has absolutely no doubt of its authenticity. If the true facts can eventually be presented to him, however, the mechanism of his mind instantly recognises them as such. He has no trouble in accepting them, nor in dismissing his earlier fantasy.

Student nurse Margaret Hough, about to receive the greatest shock the human body can suffer and still survive, apparently retained the clearest possible image of that horrific segment of her life. It was a peaceful and pleasant late September afternoon. The day's lectures (ear, nose and throat) were over, and soon after four o'clock she left the Victoria Hospital, Folkestone, to which she had been seconded on the ENT course. She walked to the nurses' home, changed into 'civvies' and went out again to buy some food at the local shops. Though there was a cafeteria at the hostel, the liver disease that she carried through life made it more sensible for her to do her own catering – all fatty foods, for instance, were banned. The route to the shops took her through a mostly residential area and past a brick-walled roundabout. Each of the roads that led off it was marked with a zebra crossing.

'I always have this feeling that there are a lot of mad

drivers about, but if you step off the kerb and expect them to stop, you're mad as well. I try to use crossings all the time - well, I used to - and as I stood on the edge of the kerb a Triumph Vitesse came up on my right and stopped. The driver beckoned me across. Mum had always drummed into us, if someone beckons you across, don't rush out straight away: check and make sure everyone else knows you're coming. So instinctively I checked, and nothing else was about. I started to cross.'

That Margaret had made it as far as she did as a nurse was a little miracle of persistence and determination. Nursing was the only career she had ever wanted, but by the time she came to it, she was carrying a handicap: a permanently stiff right leg, the knee packed with surgical cement to replace a joint eaten away with septic arthritis. It was set with a slight bend, to make it look a little more natural, and Margaret impatiently dismisses any thought of it causing her trouble: 'Running was a pretty ungainly business, because the leg had to swing out sideways a bit, but I managed. I can honestly say it was never a real problem, and I was determined that nothing was going to hold me back.'

As soon as she was walking properly after the operation, she wrote to St Thomas's Hospital, London, for an interview to get her nursing career under way. The interview was not a success: 'The woman was beastly,' Margaret recalls with some venom. Her attitude was that with a leg like that Margaret would be a liability on the ward, and that there was no question of accepting her for training as a State Registered Nurse; at best she could only be considered for the lower qualifications of the State Enrolled category.

Next she wrote to the matron at Dover (the family lived at Orpington). Margaret wanted to know from her, honestly, whether or not she had any future in nursing. This time the interviewer was 'just marvellous'. Perceiving that the spirit of nursing ran through Margaret's veins, the matron suggested she should come to Dover as an auxiliary nurse to see whether she could cope physically, and to confirm that she really wanted to go on with it.

They put her on a light ward first, in the eye block. She ran errands, made beds, served meals, did the chores and loved it all. No problem, no pain, no tiredness. They put her on a heavy ward, and everything was still fine. She even coped with lifting patients, by working with her legs apart and the good one slightly bent (the right was more than an inch shorter than the left).

So it was as a real SRN student that Margaret Hough, in a light blue mackintosh, sensible shoes and the twenty-third year of her life, stepped off a Folkestone pavement and into hell.

'Out of the corner of my eye I saw a red Mini arrive behind the Triumph and I knew I was going to get it. It came from nowhere and smacked into the back of the other car. I can see it all as clearly as anything, but all the bits seemed to happen at once.'

If we could see a slow-motion film of the incident, it would probably look like this: Margaret was half-way across the width of the Triumph when the Mini smashed into it. Possibly to try to give herself more room, and possibly to try to protect her stiff leg (she had been warned that if she broke it, it would probably have to be amputated), she turned away from the car. She was thrown into the air and when she came down the base of her spine hit the kerb. She fell forward into the road and was run over by the Mini. The Triumph came to a halt clear of the crossing, with two burst rear tyres.

'I can remember terrible pain, in my neck and up over my head. There were waves of misty consciousness, and if anybody had asked me what my injuries were and I'd been able to answer, I think I would have said my head must have cracked open. I remember someone saying something about "Sit her up", and I knew that couldn't be right. I don't know what else there was, only the pain. The next memory is the x-ray table and a terrible burning sensation on my face. I don't know why, but it was very strong. Then there was the awful part, tubes being stuffed up my nose, and being prepared for operations.'

The driver of the Mini, an Italian, did not have a licence on him. As is customary, he was required to produce it at a police station within twenty-four hours, but failed to do so. When the police went to the address he had given, his landlady said he had disappeared, owing her money. The same day his car was stolen from the police pound, and neither the man nor the vehicle were ever seen by the police again. The driver of the Triumph said the Mini had been following him earlier and that the driving had been so erratic he tried to let it pass him. When the car was lost to his rear view mirror, he presumed it had turned off – until, like a thunderbolt, it hit him.

The monstrous sum of the devastation to Margaret was not for some time apparent. It seems possible, to put it lightly, that the treatment she received in the first two of the three hospitals in which she passed most of the next year was inadequate. Margaret is sure that the doctors concentrated for too long and too narrowly on the most urgent, life-saving operations to mend her severe and widespread internal injuries, and gave insufficient attention to the spinal cord damage ('I kept telling people I couldn't feel my feet, but they didn't seem bothered'). When she left the Folkestone hospital two months after the accident, she still believed she would be returning there as a nurse.

Her pride in that job remains immense and shining. With naïve simplicity she will say, and often, 'Nobody can say I didn't do it, because I did. They can't take that away from me.' She belongs, by nature if not in years, to the old school of nursing; to the days when nurses were expected to be proud, dedicated and selfless. Today she is caustically critical when she sees lower standards of nursing and of discipline, and on behalf of what will always be her calling, she is ashamed.

'The matron at Dover was in some respects a bit old-fashioned, but she had all the right values. I tell you what, if you met with her approval, you could call yourself a nurse. My great mate there was Kwai, a Malaysian girl, and we went well together. We didn't care what we had to do. You know, in nursing there are some jobs that are not as pleasant as others, and there are some people who will go to all lengths to avoid doing them. There were two who joined with me, much younger than I was, who always tried to skive off from the worst jobs, just weren't around when they came up. That's not nursing. Kwai and I just got on with whatever came up and found a way of enjoying it all. It was a hard life, you can't get away from that, but I didn't find it as hard as life at school, for example, because that I did not enjoy. I loved nursing so much I can't imagine I would ever have found it hard. I loved it all, and I'm sorry that now there seem to be so many so-called nurses who don't love it, who look on it as just any old job.'

The devilment that has always been an integral part of Margaret's nature – and that doesn't change when you sit in a wheelchair – had plenty of opportunities for exercise when she was a student nurse. She hugely enjoyed the scene when the girl given the job of sterilising the thermometers did so by putting them in boiling water; and even more, the night the young student was told to collect the false teeth for cleaning, and collected them all in the same bowl: 'We had a lovely job that night, tip-toeing around the ward trying to match up the teeth to the faces. It's not easy.' Most of all, she enjoyed Mrs Smithers.

Mrs Smithers was the name given to the dummy that serves as a patient for the junior students. She is supposed to be everything a human patient should be, except alive.

Students are taught to treat Mrs Smithers with respect, and to minister to whatever needs the staff decide she has from time to time. If Mrs Smithers needs feeding, she must be fed; if she must have an injection, an injection she is given, wherever it is called for. She is used to help teach the students how to make beds, turn patients over, give them blanket baths and so on. The dignity accorded to Mrs Smithers and the sense of humour allotted to Nurse Hough collided one rapturous day. The young lady visited a joke shop in Dover and bought one of those extremely nasty and hideously realistic, glistening items known in the trade as a 'dirty Fido'. She thought it would be rather interesting, perhaps illuminating, to find out what would happen if she put it in Mrs Smithers' bed. What happened was that the sister tutor pulled the bed covers back and screamed. 'I was never sure what happened to it,' said Margaret, 'whether it went through the laundry or what. I didn't claim it.'

Mrs Smithers didn't seem to mind, and a few weeks later got Margaret out of trouble. Late for the afternoon lecture on the very day the tutor had admonished the students for unpunctuality, Margaret rushed in and said, 'Quick, Sister, Mrs Smithers has had a heart attack.' The students had to run out and act appropriately, and Nurse Hough was commended for her initiative.

Margaret was never going to rush into a room again, though in those two months as a patient in Folkestone she didn't know that. Incredibly, she had broken no limbs in the accident, though she had a lot of severe sprains and grazes. Out of sight, she was a mess, with very heavy internal bruising and bleeding, splits and ruptures, and damaged lungs. There were two operations in the first week, but significantly her most vivid memory was, when they were over, of the nurses trying to prop her up in bed and being surprised that she kept flopping over. Internally, she was fit enough to be transferred to the family's local general hospital at Orpington at the end of November. She left Folkestone without anybody mentioning, in her presence, the word 'paralysed'. Never having done any specialised nursing of spinal injuries – few nurses do – she did not recognise that the harsh problems of bladder and bowel that she was experiencing were typical of paraplegics; and if anyone else in Folkestone knew, they certainly didn't tell her.

It is easy to be sceptical of Margaret's litany of complaint against the medical profession for the sins and omissions of care that she experienced during the next two or three years. It seems sometimes that her judgement has been overwhelmed with bitterness, that there must be room for adjustment and compromise in her criticism. On deepest reflection, that appears unlikely. The totality with which she adjusted to the ghastliness of her trauma as soon as it was fully comprehended, the sanguine attitude with which she has faced and overcome each new disaster, and her absolute lack of bitterness towards the world in general all indicate that when she says she met a fool, then a fool was probably what she met. Those of us who have had unfortunate experiences with comparatively insignificant medical and physical malfunctions may recall the acidity in which we held them. How might we have regarded such a fate as befell Margaret?

'I always vowed after my accident that I wouldn't say, "Why me?" What does that mean – that it wouldn't matter if it was your neighbour or the bloke down the road? I can honestly say I've never asked that question. It was me and that's all there was to it. I took it on from there. The world doesn't owe me anything special: I owe it thanks for having me.'

It seems unbelievable in the circumstances, but when Margaret was transferred to Orpington, she did not go directly from one hospital to the other. She was first taken for a few days to her home at Lullington Crescent, St

Paul's Cray, and how her mother coped even temporarily with the appalling problems that visit presented is hard to understand. At Orpington General, they operated for the first time on Margaret's back, shortly after what she described as 'definitely the worst Christmas I've ever spent'. She was in traction, a 40lb weight on each leg, the bed tipped up with her head down. The surgeon found a load of discs shattered in the lower part of her spine, and thought the best thing to do, said Margaret, was to remove the odd lumps and bits that were hanging about. 'I think he realised I was paralysed, but he wasn't going to admit to me that I was. I still couldn't feel a thing in my feet and legs.'

Fourteen days after the operation, they took the stitches out. The wound, which had been oozing, promptly burst open again. Two weeks later, there was still a hole in her back, and they took her to the operating theatre again. Again when the stitches were removed, the wound burst. Margaret knows now that no wound, however slight, heals easily in an area that is paralysed, but nobody told her that at Orpington either. The feeling was growing on Margaret that if something was not done about it soon, she was going to turn into a human cabbage.

In the Spring of 1974 Margaret and her mother managed to get her admitted to the Brook General Hospital at Shooters Hill, Woolwich, where there was a regional neurosurgical unit about which they had heard from a friend – an ambulance driver whose back was squashed when the wind blew the ambulance door shut. The day she went there was the day she started to go forwards instead of backwards. There the surgeon told her, unequivocally, that he couldn't cure her, but he would try to tidy things up a bit: she had, he said, been left in quite a mess.

Margaret was sure by then that she was to some extent paralysed, and that her nursing career was over, but she did not fully understand why. Without pretending to possess anything but the crudest knowledge of the human frame, it is necessary for us at least superficially to investigate what may happen when the spinal cord is damaged – and, indeed, what the spinal cord is. Up the centre of the thirty-three separate vertebrae that form the spine, from the base of the skull to the coccyx at your tail, runs an unboned hollow about as thick as your little finger which is filled with the spinal cord. This forms the lower portion of our central nervous system, the highest and most crucial part of which is in the brain. The spinal cord primarily conducts nerve impulses to and from the brain and the rest of the body, but it also receives and originates such impulses. There are, for instance, twice as many nerve fibres emanating from the spine to various regions than there are nerve fibres running from the brain to the spinal cord; thus damage to the spinal cord does not necessarily mean complete loss of function to the bladder and the bowel, for example, the immediate governors of which are located in the spinal cord.

The brain exerts a controlling influence over the nervous system within the spine, and before any incoming sensation can produce an effect on the consciousness, it needs a clear passage to the brain. Thus if you pour a kettle of boiling water over Margaret's legs – as she once did – the message will never get to her that it hurts; but it will scald her locally as thoroughly as it would scald anyone else. Thus too, though the nerves within the spinal cord can register the imminent need to evacuate the bladder or the bowel, the warning time for Margaret is disturbingly much shorter than it is for most of us. Severe damage to the bones of the spine is almost certain to result in damage to the spinal cord within it, either by compression or laceration or both, and at the moment there is little chance of repairing that damage (though, experimentally, a remarkable degree of success has begun to be achieved). The problem is that, as with most experiments on delicate and critical functions, including the heart, the choice may be between the possibility of success and the tragedy that may accompany failure.

To what degree the nervous system ceases to function when the spinal cord is damaged depends largely on the precise position on the spine at which the damage occurs. By the time the spinal cord has reached as far down as two vertebrae into the lumbar region, it has tailed off into a collection of threads (the *cauda equina*), damage to which is likely to affect only the buttocks and the legs. The small of the back is a point where the spinal cord is frequently injured, where the first lumbar and the twelfth dorsal (or thoracic) vertebrae meet. The thoracic area runs from there up behind the chest to the junction with the eight cervical vertebrae at the neck. Life is in danger if these are broken, and bad damage to the cord above the fourth cervical nerve often results in instant death.

A break in the neck a little lower than that, between the sixth and seventh vertebrae (with the usual attendant damage to the spinal cord), brings paralysis to almost all the muscles of the trunk, as well as the legs, and a corresponding loss of feeling. The shoulder muscles usually retain power, as do those of the biceps (which bend the elbow) and the wrist extensors (which bend the wrist backwards). The numbness of the trunk, which is so complete that there is commonly no sensation when the flesh is subjected to pinpricks or even flame, may extend to the fingers and hands, and the inner surface of the arm. Though the diaphragm usually continues to function, breathing is greatly hampered by the paralysis of the chest muscles. Any cervical lesion (the familiar medical term for injury) is also likely to damage the function of the autonomic nervous system throughout the whole body – that which is concerned with the function of the involuntary muscles (those not under the command of the will) and the internal organs.

The effect of damage to the thoracic vertebrae and its corresponding section of the spinal cord will be the more severe the higher it is, and will vary according to what part of the cord is damaged. When it is disease rather than injury that has affected the cord, it often happens that a section and not the whole cord is affected. What the doctors call the posterior part of the cord (the back of it) controls the function of sensation. Disease there means that a condition of ataxy may be produced and the patient, though he may retain strength, can't control his movements because he doesn't know the direction his limbs are going to take until he sees them move. If the anterior of the cord is affected (the front), then it is not the messages from the limbs to the brain that are stopped, but the other way round: the impulses from the brain cannot reach the muscles below the damaged area, and so their power of movement is abolished. If disease has attacked the lateral portions of the spinal cord, from which the controlling motor paths from the brain run, then some degree of spasticity may result: when the muscles contract, they do so excessively, making freedom of movement impossible. Ataxy and spasticity are both groups of cerebral palsy, many sufferers from which take an active part in sport for the disabled.

In the case of injury rather than disease, the whole thickness of the spinal cord is likely to be damaged, and all the functions of the body below the point of injury will suffer, often to the extent of total paralysis. The nutrition of the paralysed parts tends subsequently to be affected and bed sores (or, more properly, pressure sores) result. This condition is not as trivial as it sounds: it is the greatest threat to the chair-bound or bed-ridden patient and if not carefully treated can lead to death, and in the past often has done. Like any other surface injury on a paralysed body, sores are very reluctant to heal and sometimes never fully heal, despite the most devoted treatment.

The formation of these terrible sores (also known medically as decubitus ulcers) is through a process so simple and so inevitable it is maddening. If you, a normally healthy person, were to sit or lie in exactly the same position for hours on end, without any movement, the same thing would happen to you: the blood supply would be cut off to the area of your flesh that you are compressing against the chair, and so therefore would its essential supply of oxygen. Without it, the tissues die and decompose, and a discharging ulcer is formed. It never happens to the rest of us because pretty soon the discomfort of sitting on that one spot becomes painful, and we adjust our position. The blood flows again to the affected area, and all is well. But for the paraplegic, there is no surface pain. He doesn't know what is happening to him until it is too late.

You know very well where you would be likely to suffer from prolonged sitting, because you can feel those two bony lumps that first meet the chair when you sit down; and in bed, it is similarly bony areas, particularly when they are not protected by much flesh, that are in danger: the backs of the heels, the outside of the ankles, the back and sides of the hips, the outside of the top of the thighs. In his first weeks at a hospital like Stoke Mandeville, the patient will be turned in his bed every two hours day and night, so great is the nursing concern about pressure sores. Later, the patient will be expected to move himself, if he can, every three hours. When he is in a wheelchair, he must at first raise his bottom off the chair (even with its sorbo rubber cushion or sheepskin) for at least ten seconds every three minutes, and later, every ten minutes. In the end, it must become a subconscious habit. Even the involuntary pressing of the leg against a hard object can produce a sore, or clothing that doesn't fit properly, or (certainly) not noticing that some small, hard object has slipped down from the lap or the arm of the chair and become wedged under the thigh.

Paraplegics are urged every night to examine their bodies minutely to see that there is no sign of a red patch, the customary overture to a pressure sore. If there is, it must be treated immediately and no pressure must be applied to that area again until the redness has disappeared. 'This may seem a rather drastic measure,' wrote Dr J.J. Walsh when he was Sir Ludwig Guttmann's deputy at Stoke Mandeville, 'but the results of not treating the earliest signs of a pressure sore can be so devastating that the small amount of inconvenience is well worth it. It is no exaggeration to say that sitting up for one further day on a reddened seat may well result in two or three months in bed in order to heal a pressure sore.'

Like all paraplegics, Margaret dreads the beastly things, and has often suffered from them during her spells in hospital – and has even suffered, as we shall see later, from the attempts of hospital staff to cure them. But at this stage in her hospital history, that was comparatively irrelevant. The surgeon at Brook Hospital discovered that she had fractured her spine in three places, producing complete paralysis on the right from the fifth thoracic vertebra (T5) and on the left from the fourth (T4), making her a Class 2 paraplegic. An incomplete lesion was diagnosed in the area of the third cervical vertebra (C3), weakening the left arm. It was here in which, in 1981, meningitis cruelly struck to bring an end to her athletic efforts.

Such details were not immediately made known to Margaret, even in the more enlightened atmosphere of the neurosurgical specialists at the Brook. What immediately happened there was that Margaret was confident in the surgery, the nursing and the physiotherapy, and perhaps the last above all. After another spinal operation at the Brook, she began superficially to heal, and greater effort could be put into getting some bits of her back to work. Tom, her physiotherapist, was a totally blind man who soon forged with her a strong and hugely valuable bond. It was Tom who, with the surgeon's approval, at last told Margaret she would never walk again. It was to him that she was able to make the response that sets the able-bodied spine tingling: 'Give us a wheelchair and let's get cracking.'

The knowledge of her true predicament, which she had long suspected, came as a relief to her. Freed of suspicion and uncertainty, she could concentrate on progress, on discovering what it was then possible for her to do, and what it might be possible for her to do if she worked at it. Tom knew she was disabled and she knew he was disabled, and they respected each other for it. Sometimes he, blind, would take her, paralysed, for a walk. He had never done such a thing before, but each trusted the other not to let trouble strike. One could not walk and one could not see: a really crazy situation, admits Margaret, but really fun.

'It was Tom who taught me that disabled people are bloody-minded. I didn't really appreciate what he meant at the time, but I do now - and I suppose so does anyone who knows me well. One day he came in with a gash on his forehead. He'd got a bit cocky, not felt properly where he was going, and had walked into an open casement window. "You're going to learn like that one day," he said. "You're going to try things and you're going to come unstuck and that's when you have to accept that you're disabled and there are some things you can't do, you'll never be able to do."

'It was Tom who got me a proper wheelchair and got me going the right way. I realised that from then on I was going to have four wheels instead of two feet, and I started to work out the best things we could do with them. I already knew that I wouldn't nurse again. Even before anyone said anything sensible, I knew there was no feeling down at that end and that there wasn't proper movement up here, particularly with the left hand. I couldn't always get it to the right place, and when I did I couldn't always pick up what I was after. All right, my nursing career was over, but at least I'd been there. Most people have a traumatic change in their lives of some sort – starting school, changing school, exams, first job, second job. Well, I'd never felt any of that. I didn't bother at school and I never got het up when I first went to work, so I think perhaps this was my traumatic change. I'd done a lot on two feet and now I had to try and do it on four wheels.'

Some time after the first operation at the Brook, they let Margaret go home for a weekend in her wheelchair, and she made a bit of progress and life was, she decided, grand. She went in and out of the Brook for quite a while, a time at home, a time in surgery, until one day the surgeon said to her: 'Your life is what you make it now. We can try and look after the bits that work, but we can't give you back the dead bits.' She told him the family had booked up for a holiday and she wanted to go with them. Go on, he said, and do what you think you can do; but take care.

On the last Friday of August 1975 she left hospital. On the first Wednesday of September, in a public pool, she went swimming.

3 A Rag Doll

When she was three, Margaret went head first down a water chute and was disgusted when her elder cousin dived into the pool to save her. She probably should have been born a tadpole and, if she comes back, she'd enjoy that – though she deserves to be a dolphin. For a girl born well inland (St Paul's Cray, Orpington, November 1949) she has always had the most amazingly friendly relationship with water. Only with such life-long confidence could she have done what she did in the Carnbrae Leisure Centre, Perranporth, that first Wednesday of September, 1975.

They had gone down to Cornwall – her mother, brother Colin and one of the male cousins – in two cars, to stay in a chalet the door of which proved too narrow to take the wheelchair (the first of many such doors that Margaret was to meet through the rest of her life), so that she had to be carried in and out. Let's go swimming today, she said to Mum, and Mum said that'd be nice; but on the way in the car she was very quiet – unusual for Mrs Hough. It never occurred to Margaret that she might not be able to swim, that in the two years since her accident she had not even had hydrotherapy. The tiresome business of undressing and costuming her accomplished, they wheeled Margaret to the edge of the pool and unbuckled the rigid body jacket without which she could not even sit upright. The boys lowered her into the deep end and she went under.

'From where I was completely paralysed, in the chest,

it was like a solid weight. I wasn't scared, I'm not sensible enough to be scared, but as I came up I could see the relief on Mum's face. It was only then I realised that I hadn't known what was going to happen. I relaxed, swam about a bit and it all went beautifully. The only trouble was that as soon as I slowed down, I began to sink, but considering everything I did pretty well. Then Mum came in too and began to enjoy it. When we got out the attendant said, "I can see you've done that before," and Mum said, "No she hasn't, it was the first time." '

Years later, during her *This Is Your Life* television programme, Eamonn Andrews asked her mother what she had felt as Margaret disappeared under the water. 'I said, "Please God, let her come up," ' said Mrs Hough, 'and when she did I burst into tears.' She washed the tears away before Margaret could see them.

'I didn't see why I shouldn't be able to swim,' said Margaret later. 'I had full power in my right arm and quite a bit of movement in my left.' It wouldn't have been enough for most of us to risk it, but as Margaret freely admits, she has always been mad. More pertinently, she has always been blessed with a mother whose good sense and tolerance and devotion should put her in line for canonisation. A lot of parents would have said no, you can't do that, but Mrs Hough and her daughter had talked for hours about the whole situation that confronted them for the rest of their lives together. 'She realised,' Margaret said, 'that the only way I was going to be able to cope with it, and she was going to be able to cope with it, was for me to carry on as much as possible as before, and not to hold back in case I couldn't do things. I was very lucky with my Mum – after all, I was the only one at that pool who *knew* I was going to come up.'

There may not have been a more important moment in her life than that one. It was the instant confirmation that her life was not over just because she was paralysed, that all she needed to do was to fight and try and try again and she would succeed, and that is how she has lived from that day. She was lucky in that swimming had always been one of the loves of her life, and now it became her life-line.

Her life began on a council estate in Kent. Her father, a building site carpenter most of his life, came from the Midlands, her mother from London. They met in Folkestone when he was in the Army and she was working in a hotel. Margaret's sister Jean, eight years older, was born in Tunbridge Wells; her brother Colin, four years older, in Brighton. Her three cousins were boys, and Margaret's natural inclination towards football and tree climbing were well exercised. The day she first went to school, her mother took her. When she met her in the afternoon, Margaret announced that, being now a big girl, she didn't need such molly-coddling and she never had it again. At junior school she played football with the boys and was the official scorer for cricket, and those years passed without much concern. Senior school was something else: there appeared to be a requirement to work, and to work exactly along the lines laid down for her, and such a philosophy was never likely to bear fruit on that independent tree.

'I loved sport and the end of class, and I hated everything else. They didn't do enough sport, and in my time I was always trying to make it more competitive. In my last year I was captain of hockey, netball and rounders. I think I passed some exams, but I wasn't bothered whether I did or not. I was always struggling in the classroom, but I don't think it was because I was really thick – just that I wasn't in the least interested! I think I could probably have done it, but I wanted to do it my way and that didn't always suit the teachers. I've always been an obstinate pig.'

Outdoor activities, including the Girl Guides, were her passion. She belonged to a swimming club at Eltham, and developed such a powerful breaststroke that she became one of a team who used to go down to Dover Harbour at night to train to swim the Channel: 'Those nights were marvellous, really exciting. In the sea my breaststroke was stronger than the front crawl that some of the men used, and that really narked them! I loved it. There was nothing better. I was really looking forward to the challenge of the Channel – anything that pushes me to my limits, that's what I need.'

It never happened. At sixteen, she left school and went to work at the massive Shell Centre, by the south side of Waterloo Bridge – a building even bigger than it seems, as it goes on and on underground. She had long since decided that she was going to be a nurse, but even if she had been able to stay at school till she was eighteen, she wanted to spend some time out in the world before she went into nursing. Shell trained her as a key punch operator and she took her zest for life with her. Everything was good: travelling up in the rush hour was good, and travelling back home in the rush hour was good. The people were fun, even the work wasn't bad – and down in the basement was a swimming pool! Could life be any better?

Margaret wouldn't ask 'Why me?' after the accident, and says she never has done, but it is a question that must have trembled on a few other lips. Not long after leaving school she began to be conscious of a pain in her right knee. It hurt when she was swimming and when she was running and when she played hockey, and it began to be annoying even to a girl for whom discomfort is clearly not a major obstacle. 'Never mind, it'll be gone by tomorrow,' she used to tell herself; and then it wasn't gone any more and the next week it was worse and something had to be done about it.

Medical opinion decided it was a cartilage problem, but before they could operate she developed a deep-vein thrombosis in her right leg. As it began to move about her body, anxiety became acute ('A clot within a clot!' she repeats gleefully) and she spent ten weeks in hospital at Sidcup. That dispersed at last, they operated on the cartilage. The operation was not successful. The wound ulcerated and caused worse and long-lasting problems. She went to another specialist, who was not eager to interfere with what seemed to be another doctor's mess. In the end he removed what appeared from the front to be a perfectly good kneecap, but which was at the back just a soggy mess which had been crumbling over a considerable period. And as Margaret indelicately put it, 'The crumbs had been dropping down my leg!' The cleaning-up job was not sufficient. She spent weeks on crutches, with the bone sliding out of the joint every time she put weight on it, before it was discovered that her basic and chronic problem was septic arthritis - a disease that had not been considered because it was rarely found in a person so young.

The specialist was astonished: 'Have you ever knocked your knee?' he asked the girl. 'What a question to put to me,' said Margaret fifteen years later. 'Tree climbing, football, hockey, rock climbing, riding on the back of boys' bikes - had I ever knocked my knee!' So much of the bone had been eaten away that it was not possible to insert an artificial joint, and the decision was taken to stiffen the knee permanently by packing in surgical cement. In view of the joys that comprised Margaret's life, you might think that would have been no more acceptable than giving a pianist steel fingers, but as we have seen, she swept the obstacle aside as she hooted down life's path.

One doesn't want to get too morbid about Margaret Price and her ailments - and even if you wanted to she wouldn't give you much chance - but that was not the end of her teenage troubles. In their efforts to restore full circulation to her right foot before they bunged the cement in her right knee, the surgeons opened her up in the area of her stomach - and let's not even contemplate what they were doing in there. It did the trick for the foot (which she

was accustomed to seeing in shades ranging from mauve to black), but soon afterwards the young lady complained of severe digestive problems.

It was the liver that seemed to be the culprit, and a specialist put his finger on Gilbert's syndrome, a complaint so rare that your average GP knows little about it. Gilbert was a French physician, born in 1858, who specialised in liver problems. If medical language fascinates you, it may be worth reporting that someone suffering from his syndrome has chronic non-haemolytic unconjugated hyperbilirubinaemia, and nothing worse than that. That roughly means that your blood is carrying too much bilirubin, a red pigment in the bile that is associated with jaundice. This has ever since affected and controlled what Margaret can eat comfortably - that is, without pain or sickness - but fortunately it seems to allow her a reasonable diet.

She had been away from her work for so long - more than six months - that Shell politely suggested it would be better to forget about coming back. Margaret had actually not been thinking too much about it: other matters were occupying her attention.

'Once the knee was stiffened and the pain had gone, I was determined nothing was going to hold me back. I made good progress, but when they first put me on my feet I kept falling over. They hadn't told me the right leg was shorter than the other. I vowed I was going to give them back the crutches long before they expected them, and I remember promising my brother, who was in the Army, that the next time he came home on leave I'd walk to the garden gate to meet him without them. He did the dirty on me by coming home much sooner than he expected, but Mum always taught us that a promise must be kept. As he came walking down the road, I left the crutches at the front door and walked to the gate - the first time I'd tried. It was only six weeks after the operation.'

Her attitude was the truly natural one: that as long as she stayed on crutches and just swung the leg along, nothing in the leg was learning to work. The sooner she could get the muscles back into action, she reckoned, the sooner she would master the problem of walking with a stiff leg. Indeed, as she keeps saying, it never was much of a problem at all. She even learned to swim with it, though it was clear that she was never going to cross the Channel. Had that afternoon in Folkestone never happened, had she been five minutes later going out to do her shopping, she would now be stomping around some hospital ward as a staff nurse, setting fearsome standards for the students and jollying up the patients no end. Heart attacks would be hovering as 'dirty Fidos' were slipped into bed beside elderly patients and in the surgical ward stitches would burst like waistcoat buttons as she tried to keep a straight face under the Sister's wigging. Oh, it would be no misery to be under that staff nurse's care. She would have been enjoying it too, her nursing ambitions would have been fulfilled, and she would have retired happily at the age of thirty-eight when some cheerful long-term patient could not face the thought of going back to his bachelor pad without her. Three cheers for Staff Hough and let's all put a quid in the hat and buy her an electric toaster.

And yet, and yet. . . . What would the world have missed? What would she have missed? That tragedy that consigned a lively young body to the ranks of the permanently and dreadfully disabled opened doors in her life – and the lives of others – that allowed the sun to shine more brightly than it had ever done before. Thrown into a black and gaping hole, she expanded to fill it with light. Her courage has been well publicised, though it is a quality she hardly recognises in herself. Her greatest achievement has been to demonstrate to others – and not just the disabled – that there are no problems that cannot be overcome, no handicaps to which man cannot adapt. How awful it is that Margaret Price should be paralysed; yet what a loss it would have been to the rest of us if we had never seen what happened after her useless, uncontrollable body was lowered into a swimming pool, wise-cracking till the water spilled into her mouth.

'I'm the original, living and talking rag doll.' Then, explaining the little miracle that was to come: 'It all sort of hangs down until I get up speed, then the faster I go the straighter it streams out behind.'

The way of God, if that's what it is, sometimes seems strange indeed. You may wonder whether Margaret did indeed 'turn to God' after her accident, as many do in such extremity. Perhaps that would account for her shining faith? 'No, I didn't have an experience like that,' she said. 'But then, I knew He was my friend already.'

4 Getting About

By the time the family went on that holiday to Perranporth, Mrs Hough had already sounded out the local Council about moving to a house that could more conveniently accommodate Margaret and her wheelchair. There was no way that they could all carry on living under that one roof at St Paul's Cray; indeed, had Margaret been at a spinal injuries unit instead of a general hospital, it is doubtful whether she would have been allowed home from it, even for a weekend. The only rooms downstairs were one sitting-room and a kitchen, with a loo on the back porch. A family of less determination might have said the problems of accommodating a paralysed adult were insuperable, but somehow they surmounted them, not only during the time when Margaret was going in and out of the Brook, but later, when it seemed they had done all they could do for her. Her bed, of course, had to come down to the front room, an awkward enough arrangement for the others - her sister had by then gone to Australia, where she married, but her brother was home from time to time with their parents. To get her to the loo, they first tried sliding her along a board from the back door, but in the end the only practical way was to carry her out there. In May 1976, they were rehoused in a much more convenient house in the centre of Bromley, with an accessible loo and wash basin and a ground floor room where Margaret could establish her private headquarters.

It was at about that time that Margaret discovered there was such a thing as sport for the disabled - an outlet she would have found a great deal sooner had she been treated in a spinal injuries unit. Over and over again she had asked people about it, but always it wasn't really their department, she'd better try Mr So-and-So. Eventually she picked up the one name that mattered: Professor Sir Ludwig Guttmann, founder-director of the National Spinal Injuries Centre at Stoke Mandeville Hospital, Aylesbury, and chairman of the British Paraplegic Sports Society. It was to his wonderland of sport and healing and rehabilitation that Margaret wrote in the early summer of 1976, to ask if it were true that paraplegics could actually compete. She was too late to enter the National Games officially that year, but 'Papa' Guttmann invited her up to see what went on and, when she got there, encouraged her to compete in a few events. She knew that she could swim all right, and she fancied having a go at some of the field events. Though she had no experience of them, she had watched able-bodied athletes and tried to adapt their techniques to her ability.

Paralysed competitors are carefully classified according to the degree of their handicap, from the almost immobile Class Ia tetraplegic at one end of the scale to the Class VI paraplegic at the other, who has power and mobility as far as his hips. Among those who take sports competition seriously, there inevitably arises from time to time suspicion and jealousy that this one or that has been wrongly classified, which accounts for their success. At those 1976 Games Margaret, who had not been medically examined at Stoke Mandeville, competed as a Class IV para. She came away with silver medals in the 50 metres backstroke and, remarkably, in the discus - an item she had never before handled. At the end of the Games a medical was arranged and she was allotted her true lesion class, Class II - and inclining towards the strongest of Class I. Nevertheless, you could in subsequent years hear the occasional voice whispering, as she broke yet another world record in her class, 'Of course, she should be a Class III. I don't know how she gets away with it.' Physical disability, however tragic, does not necessarily purge the mind of evil thoughts.

'I found that week at Stoke Mandeville quite inspiring. It was the first time I realised that people in wheelchairs could do sport properly, could compete like real athletes without anyone around who tried to treat them like children. I was very encouraged by my swimming, because in the backstroke I beat the girl who was going to the 1976 Disabled Olympics as the Class IV swimmer: she didn't like that a bit. I'd been putting a bit of time in at the public pool in Orpington, where there was a club for the handicapped once a week.

'The discus was great, but I didn't have anyone to hold the chair, and in those days they hadn't started using chains. It was dead easy to fall out. You could do a lovely throw and plummet straight to the ground, and if you fell out of the throwing circle you were disqualified. Tough, but that's how it should be. I liked that: no messing about saying, "Ah, give her another chance." If you're competing, you keep to the rules the same as an able-bodied athlete has to.'

She came away from Stoke Mandeville full of enthusiasm and realised that if she wanted to do it seriously she would have to get herself really fit and work out a training programme – and get some equipment, which was the hardest job. She went into a lot of sports shops trying to buy a three-kilogram shot, a one-kilogram discus and a 600-gram javelin. They all, of course, thought the poor creature was potty. In one shop the girl assistant, asked to supply a discus, fetched the manager. 'A discus? Oh, I see, yes. What colour would you like?' He thought she wanted a frisbee. In the end Margaret got in touch with the physical education college at Bromley, where they not only lent her the equipment, but let her go in the grounds to train.

Though the surgeon at the Brook Hospital had told her that her injuries would never allow her to work, Margaret wanted to investigate the possibilities of training for some kind of job. Down near Exeter there was a college, St Loye's, 'for the Training of the Disabled in Commerce and Industry'. The surgeon suggested she should try and get on a course there and see what went on. She did. She didn't like what went on: 'Training for the disabled? If your disability enables you to walk and run, and preferably play cricket and football and drink gallons of beer, you'll be all right. With a disability like mine, they don't want to know you.'

There is an undisguised streak of puritanism in Margaret Price, though let us not decry that. She wants it clean and straight and honest, and she wants it sober. And like most of us, she is not happy to be ignored.

At St Loye's, she was quartered at the bottom of a hill, in a room suited to a walker, but not to a wheelchair. As a fire risk, she was in that situation a dead loss: they agreed she would probably be burned to death. Because she was not supposed to push herself in the chair out of doors, they arranged for a porter to come and push her up in the mornings, and when he didn't come, she was stuck. The strain of trying to cope with the physical demands of the place was too much for her back, and it gave way. The local sick bay could not cope with her, and she was sent back on a stretcher to the Brook. The position in which they placed her caused a pressure sore to form before she got there. Train travelling is not easy for the paralysed: on the way down, she had sat in the guard's van, with her mother beside her on a milk crate, behind the wire cage like a pair of monkeys.

The Brook treated her problems without an operation,

but St Loye's were not keen to have her back, though she had completed only two weeks of a 36-week course. She was destined for the basic six-week course in office skills, followed by a specialised course in book-keeping. In April, St Loye's said she could go back and they would have more help available for her. This time she travelled back alone, in the guard's van at the far end of the train. There was a moped in there, and the only person who spoke to her was its owner, who came to get something from it and bought her a cup of coffee. All right, there is no obligation on any of us to look after the disabled, we don't owe them anything – but doesn't that tale make you feel uncomfortable?

Back at St Loye's, she sailed through the basic office course, but there was little pleasure for her there until the arrival of a former agricultural metal worker who had come on an electronics course: his name was Frank Price. One day he gave her a push going up the hill, and then he always seemed to be there. He used to take her swimming to the Exmouth open air pool, where she began to build up her stamina again – she was determined to have a serious go at the 1977 Stoke Mandeville Games.

'One of the attendants used to help Frank lift me into the pool, and then if I was doing a distance workout, Frank would sit in the wheelchair with a stopwatch. The swimmers would come along and think, "Look at that poor old bugger in the wheelchair," and Frank would get up and go to the loo! People would swim alongside as I went up and down the pool, and when they fancied it, they would try and take me, which was very good training for me. I'd let them catch up and then I'd push ahead again, and they'd be really disgusted when they saw that I had to be lifted out of the pool at the end of it.

'They were terrific to me at Exmouth. When they lowered me in they used to ask if it was cold, but it wasn't until it got up to my armpits that I knew whether it was cold or not, and by then it was too late.

'There was a kid there one evening, about ten years old, and he saw I wasn't using my legs. Frank said, no, she can't, this is her wheelchair. So with his mates he tried to do a width without his legs, and after a few strokes he turned to Frank and said, "Hey mister, it's bleeding hard work, isn't it?" The kids are usually marvellous. They accept disability and treat you like anybody else who's keen on sport. It's their parents who often shy away from it. They think sport for the disabled means tiddlywinks.'

There was no great enthusiasm for sport within St Loye's, despite the space they had available for it, but Margaret did not let that deflect her from training for the Games. Fortunately, they were held in the week following the Spring Bank Holiday, for which the St Loye's students were allowed out from Saturday to Tuesday. Margaret took the Wednesday, Thursday and Friday off too and came back to Exeter on the Sunday with seven gold medals. The sporting phenomenon was well and truly launched. It was not easy to put her excitement behind her and settle down to the remainder of the course at St Loye's; but it had to be done, and it was prefaced by a severe chiding for her unauthorised absence, for which she was docked three days' grant money.

The efforts to turn Margaret into a book-keeper were not entirely successful, and nobody was greatly surprised at that. The most memorable day of the whole summer turned out to be the annual Open Day, when the principal played host to the Mayor of Exeter and other dignitaries, and the college was scrubbed and buffed to an almost military degree (the principal was a retired colonel). Among his plans was a one-way system in the corridors for the grand tour, with the route being marked at vital stages with white rope and posts. The temptation for mad Margaret to play havoc with the pristine plans was too great to resist. Like the overgrown imp that she is, she allowed herself to be party to a competition in which her classmates

gambled on the number of posts she could knock down on a journey to the loo and back.

She went out of the door like a tank, hit the first post a tremendous crack with her stiff leg and saw it pull all the others down like dominoes all the way to the corner. Then as she swung out to get through the loo door, which she could only do by charging at it like a battering ram, she smacked a post with the back of her chair and the whole lot went down in the second corridor. By the time she came out of the loo someone had restored order from the chaos, and to get back to the classroom Margaret was supposed to continue down the one-way system. Knowing that would be hopeless, because it went as far as the main door and up some steps, she decided she would have to go back the way she came. Stiff leg out in front, she came face to face with the procession. Very politely, they stepped back to let her by – and knocked down five posts themselves.

So much for St Loye's. But for all her dislike of the place it will always remain very special, because it brought Margaret and Frank together. It was when she came back to Exeter from the Stoke Mandeville Games, incidentally, that he met her at the station and was disgusted to see her being wheeled out of the guard's van. 'I vowed,' said Frank, 'that she would never travel like that again.' He too is a man of his word, and she hasn't.

Few of us ever give a thought to the problems experienced by paraplegics when travelling by public transport. Rule number one is, don't try. Shall we suppose you have arrived at Paddington Station in your wheelchair to catch the Exeter train. It's the guard's van or nothing, and how do you get in there? You must find a porter to find a ramp and get a hefty shove up, then you must arrange yourself to the best advantage amid the rest of the baggage. One jolting stop and you could be in trouble – Margaret once had a motor bike in her back.

The journey is unlikely to be stimulating. If you have an escort, he at best may find a box to sit on; if you don't, you're in solitary for the duration. Unless a passing passenger is kind enough to take pity on you, you have hope of neither conversation nor refreshment, and the absence of windows in the van means you're not even likely to be able to read. A visit to the loo, by the way, is out of the question from the start. Even if you could wheel the chair down the corridor, which you certainly can't, there would be no hope of getting it into those minute cubicles. It might be possible to avoid dramas of that kind on a journey to Exeter, but what about London to Edinburgh? You need an escort and you need a bedpan, and that's all there is to

it. Privacy is not provided, but you have to do without it. No, for heaven's sake don't go by train unless you're forced to.

Margaret: 'What a performance! They'd shove you in the guard's van – often not the one the guard is in – and shut the door and leave you. If you're the nervy kind it's enough to put you off travelling. You could give up quite easily, but I never let it beat me. You have to see the funny side of it or you'd sit there and cry all the way down. You feel like something in the zoo, you really do, when you're in those cages and people are passing by peering at you.

And in the winter it must have been quite difficult to make out whether I was human or not, because there's never any heating in those vans and I used to be almost buried in a sleeping bag.'

And a local journey, by bus into town? In Britain, you would laugh at anybody who raises the question. Of course nobody in a wheelchair can get on a bus, what do you expect? In some parts of the United States (and the city of Denver, Colorado, is one) certain bus routes are provided with vehicles designed just for that purpose. When the driver opens the doors of the bus and sees outside a wheelchair passenger, he operates a mechanism from his seat that turns the bus steps into a platform big enough to take the chair. That is then lowered hydraulically to pavement level, the chair wheels on, the lift rises to bus floor level, the disabled passenger organises himself into the space provided for him, the lift becomes steps again and the doors close. The operation holds up the bus for about two minutes and it is two minutes of civilised joy that somebody cares that much.

We in Britain would not like it to be thought that we don't care for our unfortunate friends. We are sorry for them, oh yes, we're ever so sorry for them. We just wish they would keep out of the way so that we didn't have to think about them. And anyway, it's a bit much, isn't it, expecting to come on buses and trains? It's not very nice for the rest of us, is it? They ought to stay at home, much better for them.

Not only does it seem that we would rather they kept off the transport, it would actually be more convenient if they kept off the pavements, out of the theatres and cinemas, didn't do any shopping and certainly never had the cheek to expect to have a meal in a restaurant (to the subject of public loos we shall return at length later).

'I never had any qualms at all about going out in my wheelchair. The use of my body had gone, but it didn't mean to me that I couldn't be seen in public places. Why should it? My life had changed, but I didn't see why it should have to stop. We soon found out that on the whole cafés and restaurants just don't want to know you, they really don't want you in. They seem to think you're going to flick peas across the table or something. But we are allowed to eat, aren't we? Have we committed some crime that means we have to be locked up out of sight?'

On the contrary, most of them (like Margaret) are the innocent victims of somebody else's crime, or carelessness; of a genetic accident or mishap at birth; of disease; or even of a medical mistake. One bonny lass who became an outstanding disabled athlete was a nurse who went into hospital for tests and came out as a tetraplegic. So should we not at least share our society's responsibility for the matter by making it possible for the disabled to enjoy a small slice of normal life?

In recent years, a campaign to awaken public consciousness to the problems of being disabled has resulted in many simple public improvements, but all too few cinemas and theatres, except the very newest of them, are prepared to put themselves out and make the disabled welcome. Far from it: the Civic Theatre in Darlington recently sent for the police to eject her!

As Margaret says, you often get the feeling that because you are disabled you are not really entitled to go in, and if you do you must accept whatever they offer you; but the Darlington case really broke the records. In January 1984 the Prices made a round trip of four hundred miles to see a fifteen-year-old Tavistock boy, Marshall Coleman, perform in *Peter Pan* – his first professional show. They ascertained first, both by phone and letter, that a wheelchair could be accommodated; received confirmation and sent their cheque.

They were given two aisle seats. Frank sat in one and put Margaret's chair close to the other. In the interval, the theatre manager said they would have to move to the area at the back allocated to wheelchairs. They tried, but the space was not big enough for the chair. They returned to the aisle, but a scene ensued, holding up the second half of the show. The manager ordered them out, the Prices refused, the manager sent for the police. The Prices demonstrated to two WPCs that the chair would not fit into the space allocated and the manager was persuaded to let her park somewhere else. He chose a space right in front of an exit door!

On another occasion, a cinema declined to allow Margaret to remain in her wheelchair in a gangway next to the exit door outside which was a ramp, because they said she would be a fire hazard; but they were prepared to lift her into a seat and take the wheelchair away. Some hope for her when the fire broke out! Because Margaret is by nature an obstinate pig, she goes on fighting; but just one experience of non-cooperative resentment is enough to dissuade weaker spirits from ever trying again.

She and Frank went once to the Dolphinarium at Brighton. There was no problem getting in, from street level, but at the end of the show the entire audience was requested to leave by one door only – at the bottom of a steep flight of steps. There was no chance of them trying that – and nor could the disabled boy and his mother who were also in the audience. They sat on, defying the repeated requests. Attendants arrived to explain that the door by which they had entered was now locked, and the key had been taken away (did somebody say 'Fire!'?) Too bad, said Margaret, you'll have to go and get it. Confronted with a stroppy Mrs Price, that is just what they did; but by then the disabled boy was so embarrassed by the fuss it was probably a long time before he ventured into a public place again.

Shopping is often no easier, and is made worse by the projecting stiff leg: 'I know it creates special problems, but there's not much I can do about it. For a start, you can't put me on the edge of the kerb waiting for the traffic to stop in case something comes by a bit close. When you get to the far side it's murder again, because the pusher is quite a way out in the road when she has to tip the chair up for the kerb, and sometimes at that point the traffic starts moving again. Mum was worried about cars going by her backside while I was worried about kicking pedestrians – specially the kind who stop and have a chat as soon as they reach the pavement, deciding which way to go.'

Going through the glass doors of shops is a hazard for all wheelchairs. If there is no third person present to hold the door open, the pusher has to turn round and go backwards. If there is a third person, it's astonishing to see how many of the public, when the door is being held open, try to scramble through in front of the chair. Once in, there is the aggravating problem of shop assistants who seem to be unable either to see or to hear the customer in a wheelchair. Why is it? What are we all afraid of? The 'Does she take sugar in her tea?' syndrome, or variants of it, seems to cause our idiotic behaviour: the uneasy feeling among the able-bodied that a paralysed person is probably simple-minded and perhaps is deaf as well, and indeed may not be able to see or to speak.

You can imagine the perils of supermarkets. It is just not possible to get a wheelchair through the narrow passage beside a cashier. The alternative in some stores is to go out of the 'In' door and come back in the 'Out' door, to approach the cashier from the rear. That is not at all a popular move. 'They talk at you as if you've just escaped from somewhere and can't possibly have enough money to pay for what you've taken.' And you get that line, so often repeated in public places: 'Fancy bringing a wheelchair into a place like this.' Fortunately, Margaret has an admirable capacity for suddenly becoming deaf when it suits her.

5 Love and Marriage

Relationships with members of the opposite sex are never likely to be 'normal' when one of the partners is a paraplegic - but who would care to define normality in able-bodied relationships? If there is such a thing, it is not a well-focussed point, but a straggling area through which runs a mean line connecting infinitely distant attitudes to love. Degrees of care, protection, provision, companionship, joy, intellectual stimulation, mutual interests and physical intimacy differ so widely across society as a whole that it would be no surprise to find a partnership involving the disabled proving as near to the truly normal as any other.

Just as a lot of paraplegic men are perfectly capable of intercourse and fatherhood, so it is true that many paraplegic women can still have babies, and do, though they may not have as much fun in the process as their able-bodied sisters. Stoke Mandeville fondly remember the girl with a complete T5 lesion who fell in love with and married a man with a *cauda equina* (low) lesion. Despite having suffered severe complications early in her paraplegic life, the young wife became pregnant and had a healthy boy, whom the parents were able to bring up entirely on their own.

Other women may theoretically have the potential to procreate, but must weigh against that act the dangers and difficulties it would be likely to produce. With a teenage thrombosis behind her, a liver complaint and a body jacket to add to her paralysis, Margaret decided against it: 'It could mean virtually nine months lying flat. You have to decide for yourself whether it's fair to try. You have honestly to ask yourself whether it is right for a baby to be born and the mother to die. I don't think it is. To me, that doesn't make any sense. But you have to take your own decision about it, just as able-bodied people have to make their decisions about things. Whether you're able-bodied or not, you have to work out your ideals and your principles and try and keep to them. I think one of the things that has helped me all the time is that I have been able to accept what I am and what I've got left, and make the very best of it that I could.'

Margaret's nature and inclinations meant that as a young person boyfriends played a less-than-average part in her life. As a child she did her best to abolish the sexual barriers and beat the boys at their own games, showing a greater interest in horse-riding, rock-climbing, life-saving and swimming than in more static teenage activities. Later, her involvement in nursing was total: 'Okay, once in a while a young doctor would ask you out and that was great, but I was never looking for marriage. You have to work very hard as a student nurse, and I wasn't interested in falling in love with the first thing that walked by.'

Frank Price didn't walk by. He tucked in behind her and gave her a push up the hill at St Loye's: 'I can't honestly say I'd noticed him before, but then he had come to college a week or two after me, and you never saw much of people who were on different courses. One night a lot of us went down to Exmouth, to the sea front, and I think then it was love at almost first sight for me. I suddenly found his company a lot more desirable than that of the others. There was someone very, very special right there, and when you sense that, it's up to you not to shut your mind to it.'

Frank himself, with a hideous marriage behind him, fell

more slowly but relentlessly under the innocent spell of this extraordinary woman. That day on Exeter station when he went to meet her and eventually saw her being wheeled out of the guard's van, he promised: 'From now on, I'll take you wherever you want to go.' It was a moving and significant moment in their lives.

Frank: 'It wasn't a question of falling in love with Margaret straight away, but there was something about her that did something to you. Other people noticed it too. I know that if she hadn't been at St Loye's I wouldn't have gone through with the course, and I wasn't the only one. I felt, well, if she can go through with it with all her problems, I'd be a coward if I backed out.'

In his lovable but temperamental old car Bessie, he took her frequently down to the pool at Exmouth. The female attendants used to help her dress and undress, and the male attendants would help get her in and out of the water. Frank began to find he wanted to be with Margaret all the time, to take her about wherever he went. An accident in her room at the college precipitated the relationship: making a hot drink at bedtime, Margaret reached too far for the electric kettle and, off balance, tipped the boiling water in her lap. She felt no pain, but knew she had to get her trousers off quickly and get a dressing on. She managed to get a nurse down to help her, but was subsequently very unhappy at the way the burns were looked after.

After work on the Friday, Frank put her chair in the car and motored her from Exeter to Bromley (175 miles), intending then to go home himself to South Cerney, Gloucestershire (another 105 miles: total, 280), and return on Sunday to take her back to Exeter – a 560-mile round trip. The Houghs wouldn't hear of it. Frank stayed the weekend with them, and from then on the romance blossomed: 'At first you don't realise what a marvellous companion Margaret is, but when you do it's difficult to be away from her.'

It was September 1977 when Frank left the college, and

the end of November before Margaret did. He used to phone her every evening and go down at weekends, sometimes to take her back to the house he shared with his mother: 'Now this is Frank for you,' said Margaret. 'The first time he took me there, he'd worked out the route beforehand so that we passed loos that I could use. Most able-bodied people, it doesn't occur to them that I can't just pop out to any old loo, but Frank had got it worked out.'

Strictly speaking, Frank is not able-bodied, or he would not have been at St Loye's. He suffers from rheumatoid arthritis, a crippling disease of the joints that from time to time holds him in such a vice of pain that he can't get out of bed. ('What happens then?' 'We don't get up, it's lovely!')

Inevitably, marriage was not a subject that could long be avoided. They were both happier in each other's company than they had ever been in anyone else's, but for both of them it was necessary that Frank should fully understand exactly what it was going to mean to marry a paraplegic. Margaret: 'Frank and I had to talk about lots of things that able-bodied people probably don't talk about at that stage, and we felt we could cope with each other. If you're marrying someone like me, you really have got to understand exactly what happens in the morning, how long it takes, what you have to do and so on.' During the summer of 1978, they spent several weekends away together, either camping or at disabled sports events.

Frank: 'There were never any second thoughts about it. Margaret was the person I wanted to be with for the rest of my life. What I had to do for her, I was doing for love. The things I was doing just came naturally, as though I had been doing them all my life. I never resented any chore I had to do: because I love her, it has all been a pleasure.

'You should remember that I was heading for a very miserable life alone. Margaret saved me from becoming an alcoholic. After my marriage ended I began to drink heavily. To try and stop myself, to fill my evenings, I went behind the bar of the social club where I worked. That was all right until the bar closed: then I would start. I was still drinking substantially when I met Margaret, but it didn't take me long to discover that I wanted to spend all my time with her. I knew this was going to be a very different marriage, one of love.'

Margaret's mother probably realised before either Margaret or Frank did what lay ahead of them. It had not been just Margaret's life that had been changed by the accident: Mrs Hough's days were full of Margaret and the wheelchair, there was barely an hour in which she could forget the ties and the responsibilities that she had to bear. She too had always faced her tasks with love and with humour, and without doubt Margaret owes much of her own brilliantly spirited attitude to the example her mother set her. They make a great pair, and when Frank came into her life Margaret reacted sensibly and sensitively to the maternal relationship. Whenever she and Frank were away, they phoned Mrs Hough at the end of the day to reassure her that all was well, and the contact has remained exceptionally close despite the two hundred miles that separate them. The weekends away that summer were a sort of trial, but it was a trial of which the outcome was never in doubt. As Margaret put it, 'Everything just fitted in, just as though it was always meant to be.'

If there are problems with a paraplegic at home, you can imagine that they are not likely to dissolve in a tent. The reactions of fellow-campers would have been worth preserving on film: 'We only had a tiny little ridge tent with a built-in groundsheet,' said Frank, 'and a plastic-covered foam mattress. The only way I could get Margaret to bed was to slide her out of the wheelchair and straight into the tent on her back. One evening when I was shoving her in by the shoulders her stiff leg caught the end of the mattress and pushed it in ahead of her. She slipped in easy enough over the groundsheet and I couldn't see that the mattress was going up the back of the tent and curling up under the roof. She was shaking with laughter all the time, but that was nothing unusual. When it fell down on top of her I had a hell of a time in there, lying beside her rolling her to and fro to try and get her on top of the mattress, and then into her sleeping bag. The tent was rocking so much it nearly collapsed and we were shrieking and hollering, and goodness knows what our neighbours thought was going on!'

There is not much doubt what the neighbours thought was going on, and when in the morning they saw Margaret's inert body and beaming face over breakfast their thoughts could have been read in the next field. The reaction was not always silent. On one of their earliest weekends, soon after Frank left the college, they were at a camp site on the Cornish coast. Frank's early morning ritual was to boil a kettle of water to wash Margaret, get her body jacket on, dress her, drag her out of the tent and lift her into the wheelchair. Just over the way was a North Country couple, the male half of which was the bone idle kind. He was sitting outside the tent reading a newspaper and observing with growing incredulity such of the Price proceedings as were visible. His wife, still in her curlers, was busy frying the bacon in the do-it-yourself kitchen extension, but when the man saw the body appear he could no longer contain himself: 'Hey Peggy,' he called, 'c'm out 'ere and look at these!'

It was during that summer of 1978 that Margaret was invited for the first time to compete in the International Stoke Mandeville Games. The Nationals are for any paraplegic to get in and have a go; the Internationals are by invitation, and Margaret's performance in the Nationals had been so outstanding that she was picked for six events: she was first in the 50 metres freestyle and the 50 metres backstroke, breaking her 1977 world record in both of them; first in the discus, second in the shot, fourth in the 50 metres breaststroke and seventh in the javelin. Not a bad performance, you might think, but not a patch on what was to come when Frank began driving her on.

They were married at the Central Methodist Church, Bromley, on 16 December - with the reception at the Church of England hall because the Methodist one was 'dry'. It was a marvellously happy occasion, for which Margaret had made both the wedding cake (square, but with the corners cut off) and her dress, a gorgeous affair of red velvet with a cape and hood ('I begrudge spending all that money on a white dress that you can never wear afterwards'). The bridesmaids were largely in black, and the guests sat where they liked in the church ('I felt that if Frank and I were there being joined together, I didn't want the rest of them to be taking sides').

The decorated Christmas tree was already in the church, and a decoration hung at the end of each pew, and when Frank turned round and saw Margaret coming up the aisle he was 'so thrilled I just couldn't speak, so I went down and gave her a kiss.' 'I thought that was really lovely,' said Margaret, blushing at the remembrance of it. The honeymoon was brief: a weekend at the Ivy House Hotel, just outside Margate. They visited the aquarium and met a shellfish called Fred. On Tuesday they went back to Bromley, because Margaret's sister Jean had come all the way from Australia for the wedding and it didn't seem fair not to be with her.

They had by then bought their house, and if you have learned anything about Margaret Price so far you will not expect it to be located in any ordinarily convenient situation. They were both in love with Devon and they were both in love with the idea of peace and privacy, and if you ever want to motor down there to find them you will need explicit directions of the most detailed kind or you may

find yourself driving in ever-decreasing circles on the edge of Dartmoor. The old cottage is not far from the Cornish border, two miles from the nearest shop, eight miles from a newsagent and forty miles from a railway station. The road outside will take two modest vehicles at a time, driven cautiously, but it's a long time since anyone saw two there at once. What happens when it snows? you may wish to know: 'It's terrific,' says Margaret. 'We're cut off.'

They had the usual ghastly time finding it in the first place: you tell the estate agents exactly what you are looking for and they send you to see something quite different. Apart from privacy, they had to have easy access into the house for the wheelchair, and a garden big enough to take the hurling of the javelin and the whirling of the discus.

Having weeded out all the property with a flight of steps to the front door, a flight of steps to the back garden, passages too narrow for the chair and gardens not even big enough for shot-putting, they had reached the stage of distress which awaits so many house buyers. Then came one they thought they would really love: in the middle of Dartmoor, with Calor gas lamps. They tried hard, but they couldn't even find it.

To cheer themselves up after that they went to Exmouth, and by chance saw in an estate agent's window a likely-looking place in Crediton. The office was closed, but off they went to Crediton in the hope of finding it. They didn't; but there in another window, amid scores of pictures, Margaret's eyes went to one simple little house. 'That's it,' she said, 'that's where I want to live.' She was right. They slept in a lay-by in the car that night and went straight to the agent in the morning. The house was thirty miles from Crediton, but it was exactly what they wanted. They were third on the list of potential purchasers, but the first man didn't have enough money and the second wasn't ready to move, and one day the agent phoned Margaret in Bromley and said if you still want it you can have it.

It's a long way from everyone, including Margaret's mother, but Mrs Hough never murmured. And Margaret, disabled, immobile Margaret, discounts distance as if it didn't exist: 'How far are we apart really? We're both on the phone and if there's something seriously wrong here or there we can be together in half a day. Do you know, when my sister came over from Australia she left Heathrom at 5.30 one afternoon and the next day she rang up to say we're home and the kettle's on. How far is that, the other side of the world, and she's there already?'

There was a lot to be done to the house, but what's the hurry? Frank has acquired a little concrete mixer and things are happening. To the left of the front door they sit and to the right they sleep, and behind there's a bathroom (sliding door, loo seat raised) and a kitchen. Margaret's terrific in the kitchen. It takes her a while, but it happens. Everything must be where she can reach it without stretching, Frank handles the pots and pans on the stove, and between them they'll turn you out a cracking meal. She chops and peels and cuts (her own hands, as well as the vegetables), and she sits long and patiently over the ironing. When that job is on, Frank is never out of the room. He can't leave her, of course, not for an hour, but then he doesn't want to, so that's no problem.

If you have an inquisitive nature, you may wonder about bathing. Margaret is quite clear on the matter: she doesn't do a lot of it. Wash basins are difficult enough, because of the stiff leg; she can't get under them, so that becomes a sideways-on operation. Bathing is a concept that, to bring it to full fruition, requires a crane driver with a hoist and a team of nurses. They tried it alone on their honeymoon – well, Frank's game for anything – and it was disastrous. The problem is that Margaret can't sit up in the bath without her body jacket, and getting that wet is not a clever idea. She has to be held up in the bath so that she doesn't slip under, but it's getting her out when the fun starts.

Lifting a semi-dead weight almost from floor level is always a lot harder than it looks, and it's worse when it's wet. Once Frank had her halfway out when he lost his balance, and they nearly landed in the bath together. Now, it's just one of a million laughs, but the rest of us should not underestimate the effort the job takes: 'It's very hard work, both for me and Frank, so we don't try it often. You feel absolutely shattered after the struggle to get in and out, and you think why on earth did I bother? It's easier, and safer, to have a complete wash-down every day, and that's what we do.'

In their life together they are quite extraordinarily content, self-contained without being self-centred; apparently as happy a couple as you could ever meet. 'I don't like the idea of these clubs and groups for the disabled, and we don't belong to any of them,' said Margaret. 'Some people get a lot of pleasure and satisfaction from them, and that's fine, but it's not my scene. My experience is that many of them have turned into clubs for "the poor disabled folk".

'We've found their members fall into two categories: people who are severely disabled, and people with a disability. It often seems to be the people with a disability who grab a lot and expect a lot and think the world owes them something. You get some of them, getting near Christmas time, weighing up which party they will go to, because at this party you get a voucher for £1 and at that one it's only 50p. I don't want to be part of that. I don't want the world to think it owes me something just because I'm in a wheelchair.

'You'll find someone who has perhaps just got a stiff leg, like I used to have, who wants to belong to all the clubs and have an orange sticker for his car and everything. Just for a stiff leg! If anybody had called me disabled then, they would have had to move pretty fast or I would have disabled them! I know I'm disabled now, and I'm not ashamed of it, but I don't think it means I've got to live and die with disabled people, and be told what I can and can't do because that's what the group does.'

Unlike most of us, the Prices appear to have abbreviated their needs to the point at which they know they can meet them – and it may not have been too difficult. They have a lot of books, to be looked at rather than read ('Mum used to despair of me, I've never been interested in story books. I'm too fidgety for that'), they play table games together, they enjoy painting and craft work of the plastic mould kind. You might expect many hours spent in front of the television set, but you won't find one there: 'Television has never interested me,' Margaret said. 'I look at it occasionally in someone else's house and I think it's awful –

the swearing's not just minor words any more, and the amount of punching and kicking and killing that goes on sickens me. I just don't enjoy it. I'd probably like to have it for sport, because they do some of that very well, but when it comes to the Olympic Games or something like that we always listen to it on the radio and imagine we're there.'

The age of the original building is lost in the bricks and mortar of twentieth-century progress, but it can hardly be less than two hundred years old and used to be a pair of tiny semi-detached homes. Each had one bedroom upstairs, and mutually the building now has a ghost – or so they say. The Prices are convinced of it. They first ran into George the night they first slept in the house, when they had a pair of friends with them. Three of them slept in one room, where they had lit a good fire, but the fourth – a man with no legs – was embarrassed to be with them. For him they fixed a sun lounger in the other downstairs room, but when Frank got up in the morning they found their friend not on the bed, but underneath it. He swore that he had been so bumped about while he was lying on it that sleeping on the floor seemed the only solution.

The idea of a ghost did not occur to them then, but they are both seriously convinced of the presence now, and neither of them seems to have any objection to it. Margaret believes he likes happiness and laughter and fun, but that he has the ability to pick people out who are not really their friends. That's when he makes his presence felt positively. There are other times when they know he is there, but he does not bother them, nor they him.

'You get a door opening, perhaps, and you feel cold air go past. When I was icing Jean's wedding cake, I thought Frank was looking over my shoulder; but it wasn't him, he was nowhere near.' When their King Charles spaniel pup, Lady, came into the house for the first time, she stood still and started to bark. The hair stood up all down her back.

'It's all right,' said Margaret, 'it's only George. He lives here.'

It was some time before either of them sorted out what was going on in the house, but when individually each of them did, neither liked to say anything to the other for fear of being thought daft. Once they both came clean, they both settled down to accept and enjoy the situation – or at least what they thought the situation to be. The only problem George creates is that he is an awful nicker of gingernuts. Once a packet is opened, they seem to disappear – and Frank swears he's not taking them all! 'I'm not saying George eats them,' said Margaret, 'but I'm pretty sure he takes them. We'll probably find a mouldy hoard of them one day.'

It would be really interesting if they found the old gingernuts behind the nineteen layers of wallpaper they discovered on the bedroom panelling, but that is probably asking too much of George. They seem to be convinced that he looks after the place when they're away, which can't be bad. They like going away, they always enjoy trips, but wherever they are the pair of them are hankering to get back: 'Can you blame us? Every time we go out in the garden we feel we're having a holiday. Do you know, a buzzard sat on that pole once. We crept along and got almost underneath before it flew off. A buzzard!'

It would be quite wrong, and clearly out of character, to give the impression that Margaret and Frank's contentment in isolation is such that, now her competitive days are past, they draw the curtains to shut out the rest of the world and moulder in their own memories. They remember with pleasure, but they look forward with joyful anticipation. 'Tomorrow to fresh woods and pastures new,' wrote Milton, and he must have seen Margaret coming. Her friends of today may call on her – if they can find her – in 1990, and it's as sure as wheels still turn that it's tomorrow she will still be looking forward to.

6 Loos in Her Life

There are loos for the disabled and there are disabled loos, and Sod's Law of Paraplegic Urgency decrees that the shorter the notice of your need, the greater the chance you can't get through the door. Worse than that, you probably won't find one at all. There is no aspect of their life in public more vital to the wheelchair brigade than this. They would swap all the theatres that provide spaces for them, all the shops that open doors for them, all the cafés that welcome them, for one good loo in every town. Thank heavens, you do see the wheelchair sign outside a good many public loos these days, but that, as you will see, is not a guarantee.

Shall we accompany young Margaret Hough on her first voyage of discovery? She was with her mother and her mother's male cousin in a new shopping precinct in Croydon. They saw the welcoming sign. 'Whoopee!' said Margaret. 'Let's go!' They followed the direction of the sign and came to another and followed that and searched and found no loo. They went back to the beginning and did it again, very carefully. Again the trail petered out without prize. They found a uniformed attendant: 'Excuse me,' said Mrs Hough, 'but we're looking for the loo for the disabled.' 'Ah yes,' he said, 'that's upstairs.'

To be fair to them, it was not actually a staircase, but a steep moving walkway. When they put the wheelchair on, it started to tip over backwards. The only other way up was by a spiral slope, so the older generation took a handle each and pushed her up. They manoeuvred her into the loo, when cousin Ron withdrew, presuming all would be well. Not at all. 'If you want the disabled toilet,' the attendant said, 'you'll have to hang on a minute. I've got to go and get the male attendant to open the door.' When he arrived, he had to climb up the outside of the loo and open the door from the inside with a broom handle. When that was done and they went in, Mrs Hough nearly had hysterics: it was impossible to shut the door while the chair was in. She managed to heave Margaret on to the seat, took the chair out and shut the door. When she came back in, she found that she couldn't lift Margaret off the low seat and back into the chair, so to help her Margaret reached up and heaved on the down pipe. When the cistern began to come away from the wall they scrambled out in double quick time.

It's not difficult to design an adequate loo for the disabled, nor is it particularly expensive. It just needs a bit of sense on the part of the architect. The door must be wide enough to take a wheelchair, and the approach from both sides must be free from tight corners. Inside, there must first be space in which to turn the chair round and shut the door (sliding doors are best of all), and secondly space for the chair to be beside the loo seat – preferably on both sides, as the most severely paralysed often only have one arm strong enough to pull themselves over. There must be bars on the walls, or a frame, or a D-ring hanging down from the ceiling strong enough to take the body weight as it transfers from chair to loo and vice versa. Neither the flushing mechanism nor the door lock must be more than wheelchair height and the loo seat itself should preferably be higher than usual, to facilitate the return journey.

There are loos like that, plenty of them, but can you get in? London Bridge Station has some nice new loos, ladies and gents and one in the middle for the disabled. But to get in that, you have to find the attendant in one of the others to come and open it. That's often the way. You have to shout and hang about and go looking, and by the time you've done that, it could be too late. As we pointed out earlier, paraplegics don't get the warning the rest of us do: when you've got to go, you've got to go. Margaret, like many others, works on a time system, going to the loo when the clock says she should. Otherwise she may not have more than a minute's warning and that's that. No time for hanging about.

'I know it seems like a joke, but that's afterwards. My own rather warped sense of humour enables me to cope with some dreadful situations, but a lot of people get so frustrated and embarrassed they just won't go out because they can't bear to face the problems, they truly dread them. I know disabled people are very often their own worst enemies, because they won't go out and live, they won't try things. The trouble is that when you do persuade them to try, they meet some problem like this and that finishes them - they won't try again.'

The New Zealand version of Margaret Price is a young woman named Eve Rimmer, who became a startlingly good field events performer after being paralysed in a car crash at the age of sixteen. Though Mrs Rimmer's spinal cord injury was of a lower lesion than Margaret's, it brought with it total loss of control over her bladder. She was able to walk on calipers, very slowly, and she reckoned she had only five seconds warning of an impending evacuation. Until, years later, she had an ileal loop operation, she faced an immense social problem:

> Every time I sat on someone's couch I was terrified that I would wet it. And I usually did. This would be a bad problem for anyone, and for a teenager it was excruciating. The fear of this happening was so embarrassing and the experience so mortifying that I was really deterred

from going out socially at all. There was no set pattern by which I could regulate my life. My bladder controlled it and that followed no pattern at all.

Eve Rimmer, from whose book *No Grass Between My Toes* that story was taken, was in that respect no worse off than many British paraplegics - particularly the women. The men have always had something on their side. It is called a kipper. A plastic bladder rather like the inside of a football is strapped to the lower leg and, via a tube down the trousers, receives the water directly from a penile sheath. When you see a man in a wheelchair squeezing his calf, he is probably finding out if his kipper is full. When it is, he can wheel himself to an ordinary urinal (as long as it is not up a step), turn up his trouser leg and turn on a tap that empties the kipper. How many thousands of women over the world have longed for a system as simple!

Meanwhile, the lucky ones who are given slightly more warning search, sometimes frantically, for a public loo that they can use. The Prices found one in Cheltenham, a special new loo for the disabled, but it was locked. Not locked so that you had to get the key from someone, but locked so that the disabled, could use a universal key to open it. The trouble was, nobody had told Margaret about it.

Charing Cross Station has a splendid system. There's a new loo for the disabled right opposite the ticket office. You go up to it and press a bell, and the bloke in the ticket office sees you're disabled, presses a button and the door opens. Inside there's a big wide room with a bed, wash basin, chairs, everything you could want; but to get to the lavatory itself there is a narrow door and a sharp left turn. They couldn't get the wheelchair in and had to use a bedpan outside. Next time they went there was a notice on the door saying 'Toilet not in use', but it didn't tell you where the nearest one was.

The Prices have a leaflet detailing all the loos for the disabled in Devon and Cornwall, which is very helpful. Some of them, of course, are only open in the holiday season; others have an asterisk against them in the leaflet. That indicates you have to go up or down steps to get to them. 'I ask you,' says Margaret, tearing her hair, 'how can you have a disabled loo with *steps*? If you're disabled and not in a wheelchair, you can almost certainly use an ordinary loo, so what's the point?'

In Exeter there's a disabled loo where the door opens at the top of a slope off a very narrow pavement. If you are trying to get in alone, you're liable to end up out in the road. And at the Limbs and Appliance Fitting Centre in the same city there is a beautiful loo for the disabled (well, if they can't get it right, who can?), but the flushing chain is so high you can't reach it from a chair and the overflow pipe is directly above your head as you sit on the throne. There used to be a smashing Portaloo for the disabled somewhere on the M4, a really good one, with loads of room. They replaced it with a permanent loo that was even better, except that, for the comfort of the users, they had put a heater on the wall in such a position that you couldn't get a wheelchair next to the pan.

In hotels (or, of course, in private houses) the disabled have no hope. At their most optimistic, they get the chair near enough for an escort to carry them in, and that raises the problem of the sexes. A mother with a teenage disabled son will feel she cannot go into a gents' loo, and the boy is embarrassed at being in a ladies'. The Prices have got over it: Frank has been in more ladies' loos than he's had hot dinners. He doesn't ask permission, he just goes ahead and takes her. He lifts her in and then stands outside the cubicle with the wheelchair. Margaret enjoys the situation: 'I hear someone else coming in the room and there's a little squeal and the footsteps stop. Then Frank says, "It's all right, you're in the right one and I'm in the wrong one," and you hear the footsteps quicken and the door shut again. One day I'm sure he'll get a tap on the shoulder and be carried off and I'll be left sitting there for ever and a day.'

She had to go to an assessment board in Harley Street once. They sent a taxi for her to Bromley and by the time they got up to London Margaret was feeling mischievous. She told the taxi driver he was not to help her out, so he went in and told them she was there. 'Fine,' said the dolly bird receptionist, 'bring her in.' 'Well,' he said, 'I'm just a taxi driver, I can't take that responsibility. I think you'd better do that.' So these three birds with false eyelashes tripped out, said Margaret, and tried to put the chair together and lift her out, and Margaret was laughing fit to bust. They hadn't a clue. They actually dropped her in the gutter, which embarrassed them a great deal more than it did Margaret.

When they finally got her down the passage and into the lift they found there wasn't room for her stiff leg. At Margaret's suggestion, they let down the chair support and held up her leg themselves, and that way they got her to the first floor. By then there was half an hour to go to the appointment, and Margaret knew she would have to go to the loo. That was the wildest circus of all, going round in circles trying to get her through the door and chipping paint off the posh corridors. The loo was minute, and after a long struggle she ended up sitting on the seat with one of the girls.

When the Prices pass a public building in the process of construction they try to nip in and see if there's a loo for the disabled on the plans: 'All we need is a bit of room, a door that will shut and something to hold on to. It's not so much, is it?' There are far more usable loos around than there were ten years ago, but the inadequacy of the provision is still insulting. With Frank's help, Margaret Price makes light of the affair, but a lot of people can't do that. Some by-pass the problem by being catheterised, but that brings a greater risk of urinary infection and of kidney problems, as well as the bother of taking equipment about.

'Nobody but one of us can understand how difficult the whole loo business is, what a major problem it can become. I know that once I start to say, "I'm sorry I can't come" because of the toilet business, then I'm going to restrict my life terribly. I think I've as much right as anyone else to go out, even if I am in a wheelchair, so we go ahead and don't take any notice of anyone else. We go to whatever loo we can find and Frank looks after me and that's that. If we get an invite, we go.

'A lot of wheelchair people make an excuse and say they're sorry, they can't come this time. What they're really saying is that they won't come because they don't know what the toilet situation is. People are less inclined to ask you out if you've said no once, and once you have said no, it's easier to say no again than to say yes. And every time they say no, the four walls of their house or their room come that little bit closer. Before they realise it, they're prisoners.'

7 Help at Hand

For centuries society at large regarded the severely disabled as outcasts. Even their own relatives often hid them from the community for fear of the shame they would bring on the family, and it took the millions of casualties from two world wars to alter profoundly our attitude towards the handicapped. Largely because medical science has in the past forty years been able to guarantee a life worth living to most of them, the State's official policy has become to provide rehabilitation, training and, where possible, employment for the disabled. The Government's humanitarian lead has not necessarily been followed by adequate caring in the community, nor by an obviously enlightened attitude from all of us as individuals. As long as we don't want to know, we shan't need to care. As it happens, that's a pretty daft attitude, because the daily domestic problems of those who are coping with a normal life despite severe physical handicap are quite fascinating to discover; and so are the ways in which, by good sense and advanced science, gadgets to make the coping easier are being developed.

Through Margaret's experiences, we have already got an idea of how a spinal cord injury causes paralysis and what are the public problems faced by someone in a wheelchair. But who else, apart from those who have broken their spine, is likely to be in a wheelchair, or to have extreme difficulty in walking? Polio is probably the best known of the paralysing diseases – properly poliomyelitis, or infantile paralysis (so called because it occurs more commonly in children than in adults). This is an acute infection of the substance of the spinal cord. It used frequently to be fatal, but seldom is now. Treatment may reverse the initial paralysis of one or more limbs, but not always. In the worst cases, paralysis is so complete that the patient can only breathe with mechanical help.

Spina bifida babies are often born with paraplegia because the spine and spinal cord did not develop properly before birth. Congenital malformations are always tragic, and this one particularly so because many of its sufferers also develop hydrocephalus ('water on the brain'). The paralysis of the legs may be permanent, but much can be done to enable these children to grow normally provided treatment is undertaken immediately.

Multiple sclerosis is another disease of the central nervous system frequently causing paralysis of the limbs. It may also affect speech and sight, and unlike polio is a progressive disease. So too are the various forms of muscular dystrophy, a disease that causes the limb muscles to waste. It is the joints that suffer from rheumatoid arthritis (the disease to which Frank Price is subject) and the inflammation can become so bad that the patient is unable to walk.

The brain is the source of the disabling conditions known as cerebral palsy and cerebral haemorrhage. The former frequently produces, as well as some mental retardation, a lack of control of the limbs that causes its sufferers to be commonly, but incorrectly, known as spastics. The latter is one of the medical terms for what most of us call 'a stroke' – a sudden interruption to the blood supply to the brain, the consequent damage to which can result in some degree of paralysis on one side of the body or the other. Recovery from such damage varies so widely, according to its severity, that one patient may die and the next completely recover.

The next time you see someone in a wheelchair, the chances are that he is a victim of either one of those disabling diseases, or of a traumatic spinal cord injury, like Margaret. All these non-walkers, from the moment they arrive back home, have to master problems that they never knew existed. Much should have been done to prepare the way by the almoners and social workers at their hospital, but as Margaret discovered, it doesn't always happen. Everybody knows that a wheelchair does not go up steps, which often poses a problem even before you get to the front door; and if you have thought of a ramp, let's hope you thought of the gradient: never more than 1 in 12, with a maximum length of ten metres and a level platform at its head - otherwise what happens while you're looking for the front door key? The ramp should be made of concrete with a slip-resistant finish, and must be not less than one metre wide.

Width of access is something that incessantly plagues the wheelchair user. Any self-propelled chair is likely to be at least two feet wide (0.61 metres), which means that doors need to provide a clear width of six inches more than that (0.75 metres) and passages should be three feet wide (0.91 metres) - and without ornament-laden occasional tables. Incidentally, a wheelchair needs an absolutely clear turning circle four feet in diameter (1.2 metres), and you don't find many living rooms with that kind of a hole in them. The tighter the space in the passages, the more certain it is that the corners will soon be damaged; and internal doors are almost sure to suffer from the buffeting of foot-rests.

The best way for an able-bodied person to discover how difficult domestic life can be for the chair-bound is to go round the house sitting on an ordinary kitchen chair and see what happens. Can you comfortably reach the light switches? How about the telephone? How many cupboards are either too high or too low, and when you can get to them, can you reach to the back of them without leaning forward in the chair? Now, what about the dining table: your wooden chair will go under it all right, of course, but would the arm supports of a wheelchair keep it out too far, and are there any stretchers under the table that would foul the foot-rest?

The kitchen brings a completely new set of hazards. From your chair, can you reach all the cooker controls, see into saucepans, use the 'eye-level' grill? How about the sink: could you do the washing-up from your chair, reach the taps to fill the kettle? And can you, anywhere in the house, open a window from your wooden chair? Can you even see out of one at eye level?

We have said enough about loos already, so for the time being we'll say no more except that if you are building a new loo for a wheelchair user, its minimum internal dimensions will have to be 4ft 7in wide by 5ft 7in long (1.40 by 1.70 metres). This allows the chair to approach the pan from one side only for the transfer, but does allow it to turn round. With a paraplegic in the house, it is more than ever desirable to separate the loo and the bathroom. In the latter, he must have unobstructed access to the wash basin, which means not only no cupboard under it, but no pipes either: remember that a paraplegic's legs will be very easily burned by being pressed against hot pipes, and he will neither know that the pipes are hot nor that he is pressing against them. For the same reason, it is much safer for the bath to have its taps at the side, where the paraplegic can feel them with his hands, then in the usual place at the end, where his feet can be scalded.

In the bedroom (which obviously has to be downstairs), sit in your kitchen chair and see how you get on with the wardrobe. Impossible? The rail will have to be lowered to less than five feet above the floor. If you are preparing to receive a paraplegic in the house, you will have been told what kind of mattress is necessary, but have you thought about the height of the bed? If he is to get in and out without help, the top of the mattress should be as nearly as possible at the height of the wheelchair seat with its cushion in it.

To anybody so disabled that he has to spend all his days in a wheelchair, independence is a very valuable commodity. Margaret and Frank Price have dovetailed their lives very finely. Their extraordinary closeness is not only rare, but would be unwelcome in many families - and indeed almost impossible to arrange if one of the partners were out to work every day. Where the disabled person is of the younger generation, it is particularly important that he should be able to free himself as far as possible from the necessary ministrations of his parents (tragically, many paraplegics are young, because of the horrifyingly large number of spinal injuries suffered by motor cyclists). So a great deal of thought needs to be given to providing a home that is both comfortable and workable for a wheelchair user.

If he is paralysed, the likelihood is that he will either be incontinent, or lacking in control of the functions of his bladder and his bowel, and however well-equipped he is with surgical and welfare help, that will remain a major problem. So will the constant aggravation of pressure sores, which have been discussed elsewhere. As these troubles can never be banished from the severely paralysed, the rest of his daily problems really do need to be eased as far as possible. Getting in and out of bed, for instance, often ceases to be a problem with a 'monkey pole' - a bar that rises from a floor stand and curves over the back of the bed, from which a chain and D-handle are suspended. The patient can take much of his weight this way, and the bar swings to the side to help him transfer to the chair. A similar operation over the bath and the loo is welcome.

Mechanical hoists of many kinds are now available. There is one that clamps to the roof of a car, to move him into and out of his chair hydraulically; there is one that will perform a similar function by the side of the bath; and there are magnificent efforts of engineering that can be arranged to carry a man in a wide canvas sling from his bed to the bath, or into the sitting-room, with the mechanism running electrically in a track bolted to the ceiling joists. Many tetraplegics, with perhaps only biceps and wrist extensor muscles functioning well, would be quite unable to live the full home life that they do without major mechanical help of this kind. Other much simpler gadgets make most moments of the day easier for them: lazy tongs, a kind of extendable pair of pincers, can pick small items up from the floor and the back of cupboards where the arm cannot reach; wooden or plastic blocks (or even bicycle handlebar grips) fixed to the handles of cutlery give awkward fingers a much better chance of keeping secure hold, and a plastic buffer can be clipped on to the edge of a plate so that awkward food can be chased against it; a light splint can be strapped to the wrist to which various everyday implements can be fitted - pen, comb, toothbrush and perhaps a sturdy pencil with a rubber end that can be used for typing.

Personal need and an ingenious mind will soon produce other aids. Many is the disabled cook who uses fire tongs to take cakes out of the oven, and some say you can wash your 'smalls' perfectly well with the aid of a large plunger (the kind used to unblock sink drains) with a few holes cut in the plastic cup. Round door handles often prove very difficult to grasp firmly, and replacing them with lever handles saves much fustration - and while you're at it, be sure they are all fitted at a convenient height. We have mentioned the height of light switches, but for someone with extreme finger muscle deficiency, many of the standard type of switches are difficult to operate. If necessary, they can be replaced with large rockers known as tip switches; with pressure switches that respond to a slight touch; or even with a switch that responds to the warmth of any part of the body that is placed against it.

In the kitchen, the carousel type of storage unit is very useful, whether it is a free-standing item for jars and pots or a wire basket that swings out from inside a cupboard or under a worktop. The backs of cupboard doors can usually be fitted with racks (much easier than trying to fish the items out from the back of the cupboard), and in the kitchen or anywhere else in the house small sets of drawers on casters are a boon. The sink unit may need some professional attention so that the wheelchair can approach it closely; electric kettles can be used on stands that tip, obviating the dangerous need to pick up a full kettle of boiling water; and taps everywhere, like door handles, operate more easily and safely with lever tops.

There are now many kinds of special baths made for the disabled. There are beautiful sit-down shower units, though as long as there is access to an ordinary shower, a plastic chair is cheaper. There's a sitting bath that looks like a sedan chair without the handles - you get in, shut the door and turn on the tap - and several more conventional shapes with seats in. On the other hand, you can buy a perfectly simple little seat that fits into a standard bath, or, for greater comfort, removable plastic bath liners of various shapes and sizes that fit into a standard bath to reduce its depth and provide security. And a few last words on loos: it's a great help if the height of the seat can be raised, and you can buy a deep plastic seat that clips over the top of the bowl and can be removed after use. If you can't get a wheelchair into your loo at all, there is a simple 'sani-chair' that you have to sit on outside; it can then be wheeled in over the bowl. And for very severely handicapped people, there's a WC that incorporates a warm-water bidet, the douche from which is followed by a long draught of warm air.

Electronic science is now producing incredibly sophisticated gadgets for the home and the office, and not only for the disabled. Push-button telephones may be a lot less difficult to operate for uncooperative fingers than the old dialling system, and it is possible to dial some calls automatically, with a pre-programmed card. For those who cannot hold the receiver, there are loudspeaking phones, and for those who cannot adjust radio controls, there is a one-switch set pre-tuned to six stations. But of all the inventions of the past twenty-five years, nothing is more stunning than Possum.

This extraordinary electronic machine, designed by the research department at Stoke Mandeville Hospital, brings life to the most immobile patient, whether bed-ridden or chair-bound. A mouth-piece with two narrow tubes, operated by very slight breath pressure - no more than can be conjured out of the cheek muscles - is capable of working a variety of appliances and services without the need for any further action. A control panel looking like a section of illuminated chessboard shows the gamut of tricks that Possum can play: light, heat, radio, television, telephone, intercom, alarm bell. It can open the front door and even activate an electric typewriter, all by a combination of blowing and sucking at one or other of the tubes. If the service the disabled person needs is the second square along the third line on the control panel, he produces the right combination of puffs to send the light down to the third line and then along one, and then he puffs it on.

Twenty years ago, when Possum was still in its early stages, it was not available under the National Health scheme. Voluntary subscriptions met the high cost for some tetraplegics, and otherwise it went only to those homes that could afford it. Today the situation has turned right round: it is not available privately, and can be supplied only on medical prescription. Nobody with Margaret Price's physical ability is going to need Possum – nor is anybody with a Frank Price to look after them – but there is something about the machine that reminds one of Margaret. Its name arose from the phrase Patient Operated Selector Mechanism, but it is not merely a coincidence that in Latin *possum* has another meaning: 'I can,' 'I am able.'

8 'Poppa'

We can go no further without turning to 'Poppa': to Professor Sir Ludwig Guttmann, CBE, FRS, MD, FRCP, FRCS, the man who was not surprisingly regarded by many paraplegics as their Messiah. Without him, the wheelchair world would even now be a very different place, and sport for the paralysed, and the multi-disabled too, might never have left the playground. It was Sir Ludwig himself who might have been speaking that line from George Bernard Shaw's 'Back to Methuselah' with which this book opened: 'You see things, and say "Why?" But I dream things that never were; and I say "Why not?" '

Dr Guttmann was one of the last Jews to leave Germany in 1938, virtually slipping out of the back door of his hospital as the Nazis came in at the front. By then he had, according to legend, saved some of his fellows by shipping them out in coffins, alive. He worked as a doctor in England through the war until, in February 1944, the British government asked him to start a spinal injuries centre at Stoke Mandeville - a hospital just outside Aylesbury, Buckinghamshire, which had won a great reputation for its plastic surgery. It had already been agreed that the best hope of furthering the study of the complex problem of spinal injury lay in specialised units, rather than scattering paraplegic patients to various general and surgical wards throughout the country, and Stoke Mandeville was not the first such unit to be established. The earlier ones, however, did not seem to have succeeded in changing fundamentally the depressing outlook of the unfortunate victims, largely because – or so Sir Ludwig thought – the medical staff at those units were only able to devote part of their time to the treatment of spinal injury patients; and because there did not seem to be any definite rehabilitation plan even for the fitter of such patients.

It is not easy for us to appreciate now, when we see paraplegics like Margaret Price driving themselves to the utmost on the athletic field, that in 1944 she would have been regarded as a hopeless cripple. A cripple without hope not only of an enjoyable, active, spirited life, but without hope of any life at all longer than two or three years. They seldom died directly from their spinal injuries, but from complications arising from them that were regarded then as inevitable: septic bedsores and infection of the paralysed bladder, resulting in destruction of the kidneys. 'The view generally held,' said Sir Ludwig, 'was that very little or nothing could be done for them and the sooner they died the better for all concerned.'

Die they did, and consequently paraplegia, unlike blindness and amputation, did not constitute a post-war social problem to the community at large. Where a paraplegic did survive for any length of time, he was kept either at home or in an institution for the incurable – the subject of charity or a focus of curiosity. Sir Ludwig changed all that; first, by refusing to believe that it was true, and then by devoting his life, and that of those who worked with him, to a complete programme of physical and mental compensation and rehabilitation for those who would never walk again. No paraplegic in his care was going to die unnecessarily.

Fundamental to his approach was that new methods of physiotherapy must be tried, even if they were entirely unorthodox. Boredom must be eliminated and the patients must be shown not how little they could do, but how much.

Within weeks Sir Ludwig had men without the use of their legs climbing ropes, using a punchball and playing darts, skittles and snooker. It seems simple enough now, but it was a physiological revolution. By the autumn he was convinced that competitive team sport must be introduced. He and the hospital's physical training instructor armed themselves with a wheelchair each and a walking stick each, and, using the curved handles, tried hitting a croquet ball and chasing it and preventing the opponent from doing the same thing.

It was clumsy, but Sir Ludwig was satisfied that he had set foot on a road that led to an exciting land. And incidentally, he suspected that in such a game as he was creating, the paraplegic might actually have an advantage over the able-bodied – a suspicion that subsequently was conclusively confirmed. Early in 1945, wheelchair polo (as he called it) was superseded by wheelchair basketball – never to return, for basketball proved to be the most exciting and fascinating team sport ever to be devised for the paralysed. At about the same time, table tennis and archery were introduced into the paraplegic programme, and the latter sport, superbly suited to the needs, proved to be the only one at which the paraplegic with good arm control could face the able-bodied competitor on equal terms; and even today it is probably the only genuine sport in which the entire outside world can be persuaded that wheelchair athletes actually take part. Sir Ludwig recalled those early moves in an article he wrote for the magazine *Archery International* shortly before his death in 1980, and what he wrote then neatly covered his philosophy regarding the whole range of sport for the disabled:

> 'It was my philosophy that sport represents the most natural form of remedial exercise and can be successfully employed to complement the conventional methods of physical therapy. It is invaluable in restoring the dis-

abled person's physical fitness - i.e., his strength, co-ordination, speed and endurance. In the contest with himself to improve his performance, the physically handicapped person learns to overcome fatigue, a predominant symptom in the early stages of physical rehabilitation, especially following fractures, amputations and paralysis.

In addition to the curative factor, sport has a great recreational value, which represents an additional motivation for playful activity and the desire to experience joy and pleasure in life, so deeply inherent in any human being. The aims of sport are to develop in the disabled activity of mind, self-confidence, self-dignity, self-discipline, competitive spirit and comradeship - attitudes which are essential for getting the disabled person out of the ghetto of self-centred isolation.

This leads to the last aim of sport for the disabled: to help him restore his contact with the world around him. In other words, to facilitate and accelerate his social integration, or re-integration.'

He took a brilliantly orchestrated step forward on 28 July, 1948, when he founded the Stoke Mandeville Games for the Paralysed. It was the day on which the first post-war Olympic Games opened in London, and on the grass outside his hospital Sir Ludwig staged an archery competition between six ex-servicemen and two ex-servicewomen from Stoke Mandeville, and eight ex-servicemen from the Star and Garter Home for the disabled at Richmond - all sixteen competitors being paralysed. Year by year this unique little celebration of triumph and joy took firmer and wider root. Perhaps carried away by its success in 1949, Sir Ludwig looked forward to the day when the event would be 'truly international, and the Stoke Mandeville Games would achieve world fame as the disabled men's and women's equivalent of the Olympic Games.'

It was not long before his optimism received the kiss of reality: in 1952 a small team of Dutch war veteran spinal paraplegics sailed across the Channel to join competition with their British comrades. The medical profession was overflowing with sceptics when Sir Ludwig launched his idea publicly at Stoke Mandeville in 1948. Such a plan was beyond reason, they said, beyond physical capability. The great man would not allow his staff to be swayed by such faithless denigration, would not tolerate the use of those easy words 'can't' and 'impossible'. He had only 16 competitors in 1948, but he had 60 in 1949, 130 in 1952 and 300 in 1956. It began to look as though he knew what he was doing. An International Stoke Mandeville Games committee was formed to consolidate the holding of the festival of sport annually at the end of July, with the exception that every fourth year the Games should be held in the same country as that in which the able-bodied Olympics took place – where that was possible. Italy took up the idea with enthusiasm, and as soon as the 1960 Olympics were over, the wheelchairs moved in: four hundred of them, from twenty-three countries.

Pope John XXIII received them all, and their three hundred escorts, in the Vatican, and made a speech which is as real and as moving today as it was then: 'You are the living demonstration of the marvels of the virtue of energy. You have given a great example, which we should like to emphasise, because it can be a lead to us all: you have shown what an energetic soul can achieve, in spite of apparently insurmountable obstacles imposed by the body.'

Four years later, in Tokyo, one of the most memorable of all the International Games took place, opened by the Crown Prince and Princess of Japan. They had a profound effect on the attitude of Japanese society to the disabled: 100,000 spectators visited the Games during the week, and within six months the Japanese government had set up a factory staffed by paraplegic and other severely disabled workers. Now there are four such factories and a fine sports centre for the disabled modelled on that at Stoke Mandeville. By 1964 the International Games were regularly attracting between 350 and 400 competitors, but there was a huge increase in the next Olympic year, 1968, when Israel held the Games outside Tel Aviv in lieu of Mexico, where the able-bodied Olympics were being held. A crowd of 25,000 attended the opening ceremony in the university sports stadium in Jerusalem, but there was something even more impressive to see on the track: a parade of 750 wheelchairs.

Out of the public eye, all was not so good. Female competitors were quartered on the second floor of a youth hostel, and seventy-two of them had to share three loos and three washbasins. To get on the first ablution shift you had to rise with the sun, and to make matters worse the door to the wash block was so narrow you couldn't get a chair through. It was when she arrived at the airport at Tel Aviv, incidentally, that the New Zealand paraplegic Eve Rimmer first realised that all might not be as it seemed when the paralysed met in competition. While the Kiwis were waiting for assistance to get up some stairs, the hundred-strong American team arrived. A bunch of them got out of their chairs, folded them and carried them up.

By the time those Games were being held in Israel, work had begun at Stoke Mandeville on the world's first sports centre for the disabled. At that time, access to public sports halls and swimming pools was often impossible for the disabled because of flights of steps, lack of lifts and the absence of adequate lavatories. At that time too – and, regrettably, still at this time – there was a psychological barrier, what Sir Ludwig called 'a prejudice so deeply ingrained in society that sporting activities of the disabled are an embarrassment to the able-bodied.' It was clear to him, particularly in view of the growing success and popularity of the International Stoke Mandeville Games, that a lead must be given to the world in the provision of sporting facilities for the disabled. In 1967 the Ministry of Health granted a 99-year ground lease to the British Paraplegic Sports Society of land close to the hospital. The cost of the lease was negligible, but £350,000 had to be raised to build the stadium and its necessary offices. With the support of the local borough and its citizens, of the Sports Council and of hundreds of commercial and private subscriptions, the money was raised in time for the official opening by Her Majesty the Queen on 2 August, 1969.

It is, in its context, a very impressive creation. Functional rather than beautiful, it offers facilities at that time unrivalled in the world for disabled athletes; and it is used not only by Stoke Mandeville patients, but throughout the year by all kinds of disabled from all parts of the country, and also as the local authority sports centre for schools and other groups. At its heart is a 12,000 square foot main sports hall with a spectator gallery for 440, and a 25-metre six-lane swimming pool with a 200-seat gallery. Two smaller halls cater for snooker and table tennis, and next door is a dining hall (for the provision of which the Round Table organisation was instrumental) that accommodates 250 wheelchair diners. Above that are dormitory units with a hundred beds for escorts.

All was not over with the opening of the stadium – subsequently named the Ludwig Guttmann Sports Centre. Five years later, at a cost of £85,000, a six-rink indoor bowling green was added that is in constant use by the local community – whose contributions to the splendid bar turn that building at least into a paying proposition. Late in 1978 work began on laying a new artificial track for athletics, to replace the old tarmac area. Another £82,000 was needed for the 400-metre, six-lane circuit, and much of the money was provided by friends in the Netherlands.

Prince Bernhard was able to open the track in June 1979; and then Sir Ludwig could turn his energies to the realisation of his greatest dream: the building of a permanent Olympic Village for the disabled.

For more than twenty-five years athletes had been accommodated in six long wooden huts that had become redundant to a friendly military establishment. Anyone who has done National Service in Britain will be familiar with the architectural style: their natural, spartan capacity would be about fifteen beds down each side, with minimal toilet facilities to one side of the hut (the lavatory cubicles had no doors, only curtains) and a small locker beside each bed – not even hanging space for clothes was provided. By the end of the 1960s, fifty or even sixty beds were crammed into each hut, necessitating a double line of beds down the middle of the room and often without the space for a wheelchair beside the bed. Bathing facilities were grossly inadequate and heating virtually non-existent – though overheating was possibly a greater danger: God knows how many might have perished in a fire.

Eve Rimmer, in *No Grass Between My Toes*, recalled her visit there for the 1970 International Games:

> 'We were bedded down in enormous army huts, sixty to each, very cramped. Clothing was draped over the rafters, and there were some of the most ancient hospital beds I've ever seen. It was in such contrast to the fantastic Stoke Mandeville stadium. This had been opened only the year before and included an indoor pool, table tennis and basketball facilities and a seven-chair lift. It was flanked by a huge marquee for fencing and weightlifting, as well as large fields, a track, a slalom course and bowling greens for the outdoor events. Everything had been designed for wheelchairs, so it was a bit like being in a paraplegics' heaven. Except that the beds weren't exactly cloud nine.'

The estimated cost of building and equipping the Village was to be in the region of £1.5 million, and an appeal for £2 million, to cover future maintenance, was launched in 1979. Enough money had been raised by July 1980 for the first turf to be ceremonially cut, and quite astonishingly the whole project was completed within one year. It is delightfully simple and very pretty, being built of 127,000 Ashfold multi-facing bricks of so mellow and pleasant a tone that one wonders why some of Britain's ghastly new housing estates cannot use them. The overall layout is of single-story accommodation built around a hollow square, but on two facing sides of the square the buildings do not meet. The other two facing sides of the square are connected by a third accommodation unit, which is approached through one of the gaps by an entrance lobby and offices. Within there is a welcome feeling of light and spaciousness, with wide corridors connecting all the rooms.

These vary from long dormitories to small square dormitories to delightful double flatlets with easily manageable bed-settees and their own kitchen and bathroom. Every one of the 424 beds in the Village's thirty-four sleeping rooms has a good locker wardrobe with mirror, and there are ample washing and shower rooms, drying rooms, a laundry room, launderette, medical centre and breakfast room. The whole Stoke Mandeville stadium operation is necessarily run by the smallest possible staff, and one of the wonders of it all is that the domestic chores in the Village are undertaken, as they were in the old huts, by voluntary labour from the community outside. There are ladies there day after day during the period of any games who have been making beds at Stoke Mandeville for thirty years.

Subsequently, the old huts were converted, as and when possible, for more appropriate uses: one is now a shooting range (for air weapons), one a weightlifting hall, one a fencing hall and one an athletics room. Two of them are also used for table tennis.

While all that work was in hand, from 1968 onwards, the International Games continued at Stoke Mandeville with higher entries than ever. Sir Ludwig deeply regretted that the West German authorities found it impossible to hold the Games in Munich after the 1972 Olympics, despite their lavishly-built stadia and accommodation: 'This shows a lamentable lack of appreciation of the place thousands of disabled sportsmen and women have earned for themselves in the field of international sport.' However, Heidelberg (the world's oldest university town) proved a superb alternative and attracted by far the highest number ever to compete in the Games. The slogan was coined there, 'One thousand competitors, one thousand winners.' Those who were lucky enough to stay in the magnificent rehabilitation centre called the *Beresfodesbundeswerk* will probably never again see such marvellous accommodation for the disabled: single rooms with baths, showers, loos and electronic doors; and with radio, intercom and push-button bedside controls for windows and blinds.

When the International Games resumed at Stoke Mandeville, the number of participants climbed past five hundred and then past six hundred, and in 1976 there were 1,560 competitors in the World Games for the Disabled in Toronto, when the wheelchair athletes were joined by other disabilities. The opening ceremony will not be forgotten by those who pushed the wheelchairs: they had to follow a display by the Mounties (the Royal Canadian Mounted Police) and their horses, and all that they left behind them. In the hope that the Soviet Union would accept the Games in 1980, Sir Ludwig went to Moscow to plead, but it was in vain. The story spread, of course, that in the USSR there is no such thing as a disabled person; but the sad truth seems to be that at that time, at least, the Soviets had experience only of the blind in relation to handicapped sport. So to Arnhem, which we shall look at in detail later, and its 2,500 athletes and the International Olympic Committee's objection to their use of the word 'Olympic'. Sir Ludwig's response was pointed: 'If you won't have us in your Olympics, we shall have our own.'

Sir Ludwig Guttmann, 'Poppa', had to die sometime. It seemed deeply sad that he could not have been spared just one more year, so that he could have seen his Olympic Village. When he went, in March 1980, a great sorrow followed him from thousands of the paralysed across the world. How many lives did he save, to how many discarded men did he give hope, from how many did he draw endeavour? Sir Ludwig altered the whole thinking of the medical world towards paraplegia, and it was to the end his dearest wish that society at large should deepen its understanding of the victims of one of the most profound of disablements. That we have at least stepped towards such an understanding is some tribute to his life's work. Would that he were here to complete it, for 'Poppa', like all great men, is truly irreplaceable.

9 In Full Flow

It was in that Quoditch garden, early in 1979, that Margaret Price really began to get her act together. It was an act that, when polished, was to prove the most successful sporting achievement the paraplegic world had ever known; but it was not universally popular. By the end of that year, she had become the best-known disabled athlete in Britain – perhaps the best-known ever – and she had stirred up a sludge of resentment. A lot of her colleagues had an epitaph ready for her: 'She tried too hard.'

As we have seen, archery had been the ideal competitive beginning to paraplegic sport; but thirty years on, with paraplegics living and succeeding in life, their sporting activity had expanded: a dozen or more disciplines were internationally practised. Some were capable of being treated only as recreational activities, if that was all that was required – table tennis, snooker and bowls, for example; and sports like archery, shooting and weight-lifting could be enjoyed privately, if necessary, in what Guttmann called the disabled person's 'contest with himself to improve his performance'. He could work at them as hard as it pleased him to do so, and to all those sports there was, and still is, no fundamental difference in the approach by the disabled or by the able-bodied: it may be a competitive approach, but it can be a recreational one. But consider the athletic events, on track and field. There is no likelihood of an able-bodied participant taking up any of them unless his competitive desire is strong: he goes in to win, or to get as close to winning as his talents allow; and even the genuinely amateur athlete is likely to devote as much time as he can to improving his performance. When a disabled athlete takes the same approach, however, there are cries of 'Unfair!' For many disabled sports people, 'playful activity' and 'social integration' mark the limits of their ambition: no harm in that, agrees Margaret, but in that case why compete in the national championships?

The dichotomy in paraplegic sport was clear and often undisguised: on one side, the many who were in it for fun and only for fun; on the other, the very few who were putting into it everything they had. Trying to straddle the gap were those who had trained themselves to the point at which they were the best of a bad bunch, and therefore candidates for the national team, but deeply resented losing their places to highly-competitive newcomers. It is a shattering truth that Margaret Price was regarded as a heroine by the nation, but as a villain by some of her comrades in misfortune. They did not make life easy for her.

'I suffered a lot of bitchiness when I went into disabled sport, because I was new and I went straight in and excelled. I was an unknown and I wiped the board, and they didn't like it. A lot of them didn't speak to me at the nationals, not even in the dormitory, and when I was about to throw they used to make rude remarks. There was lots of running to the British team manager or to "Poppa" to say I was in the wrong class and it wasn't fair, that I was denying them a place in the team.

'It was really stupid, but I let them get on with it. I was there for the sport. I didn't argue with them because I wanted to save my energy for competing. Some of them must have been in it sixteen or twenty years. I came along and thrashed them and they hated it, and me. Had I been a weaker spirit I could well have said, "Sod the lot of you if that's your attitude, I'm not coming here to be insulted." That's really what they were banking on, but I didn't give them the satisfaction of getting it.

'I wasn't the only one. I've been told by some of the people who run the sport that there were others who might have been just as good as me, but they couldn't stand the bitchiness and dropped out. To them, it wasn't worth it. To me, it was.'

Three times a week through the year Frank drove her, in the mobile bedroom that had replaced Bessie, the twenty miles each way to Tavistock. There at Kelly College, the remarkable establishment where Sharron Davies became a world-beating swimmer, Margaret ploughed up and down the swimming pool lane that was reserved for her - one of the many acts of kindness and generosity without which her talents would have been frustrated. Those of us who find swimming fairly hard work might be shamed into greater efforts if we could have seen her at it: with little to help her but one good arm and one poor one, she cut the world record in her class for the 50 metres freestyle from 66 seconds to less than 43 seconds.

(Seventy years earlier the greatest female freestyle swimmer in the world was an Englishwoman, Daisy Curwen. She was capable of about 39 seconds for the 50 metres: deprived of the use of her legs and her racing start, she would no doubt have been comfortably beaten by Mrs Price.)

Her backstroke too was way ahead of all her rivals, and she was not often beaten in the breaststroke - with which, remember, she once was going to swim the Channel. Only the butterfly was forbidden to her, the exaggerated collarbone movements of that strange stroke being a danger to her damaged neck.

It was no surprise that a swimmer as naturally talented as Margaret was from childhood should be able to outclass other paraplegics. Nothing in her history, however, sug-

gested that field events would ever be her forte. This was a little something on the side that she built up in her back garden - and something to which, no doubt, the strength of her swimmer's shoulders contributed. A vital component of the training process was Frank, anchoring the chair to the ground while she hurled. He would sit down, his legs right underneath the chair, the side of his face pressed into the back of the seat, his hands hugging the wheels: 'If I let go,' he said, 'she'd be halfway across the garden.' As Margaret discovered the first time she ever threw the discus at Stoke Mandeville, it is embarrassingly easy to throw yourself out of the chair at the same time.

Frank was not short of exercise while the garden sessions were on. With each throw of the discus, the javelin and the shot, he had to emerge from his anchor role and scurry off, like a well-trained terrier, to bring back the implement. 'And she doesn't work to any timetable,' he said in those days. 'It could be any time of day when she says, "Come on, Frank, I want to throw." We've been out here looking for the discus by torchlight before now.'

In competition, Frank had to meet the rules as surely as Margaret did. He was restricted to the throwing circle as rigidly as she was – if a bit of his tracksuit went over the edge, it was a no-throw. They were not allowed to speak to each other, so they devised a code of swings that made the message clear. Margaret could not even say 'Now!', but Frank knew when it was going, and that was when he really gripped.

'Once Frank came into my life, and got under my chair, there was no comparison in the standard of my throwing. I could just forget about the chair and let go with a full-blooded throw. He knew that if he felt the right side of the chair lifting, it was a good one. Some people get just anybody to hold their chair, but that's silly. You need to understand each other and have absolute trust in the bloke underneath. When I went with the British team to Austria the field events coach held my chair. I won the shot, but it was about a metre down on what it should have been.'

In her earliest throwing days, Margaret studied the able-bodied athletes closely, noting the positions from which the various parts of their body contributed to the throw. 'I watched Geoff Capes putting the shot. I watched his feet, his legs, his hips – everything bar the actual release. If you watch it all up to the part that you can use, then you can eliminate everything you've seen except what position you should be in at that point. A lot of people sit solid and firm in a wheelchair and expect to throw like that, but by watching an able-bodied athlete you see their hips flick and then the body starts to rotate and you must try and pick it up from there. Oddly enough, there didn't seem to be many disabled athletes who had worked that out, so it wasn't too difficult to overtake them.

'We just haven't progressed enough in our side of sport, it's ridiculous. You've got to keep up with new techniques and methods of training, just like able-bodied athletes do. But most of our people just stick to what they've always done. It was good enough then, so it's good enough now. The biggest problem I saw from the start was with those who had been handicapped from a very early age and had been to a school for the disabled where they had done what was called sport. Mostly it is so limited in those places it's more of a play-around. Playing around is fine, it keeps them happy and it's good for them, but it's an awful shame that those youngsters with talent and determination can't be shown how to make the most of it.

'You could actually pick out those who had gone to one particular school, because their technique was all exactly the same. They had all been taught the basics, but there had been no progress. Nobody had gone on to personalise the technique, to make a full-blooded effort to get better distances. I wasn't trying to prove anything to anybody, not at that stage, but I came away from my first national games thinking this is great: I like the idea, I love sport and I can take this a lot further. So I went on working it out and spending hours in the back garden trying to perfect my technique.'

It makes Margaret mad that the technical coaching available to disabled athletes was seldom sufficiently sophisticated to satisfy those competitors with real ambition – in fact she claims she never heard the British field events coach teaching technique. At the National Games of 1981 they decided to have an evening session for anyone who wanted to have a go at throwing, but the coach, she said, made no attempt to work out any technique for the individual. Most of them had disappeared inside after half an hour, but Margaret stayed out with a Welshman who was particularly keen, and taught him all three implements. They were there two hours and he was really excited. 'It wasn't that I had done anything special for him, except to work out what his physical abilities were and how he could best adapt them for the job.

'You know the symbol for sport for the disabled? It's

three interlocking rings – three wheelchair wheels – that "Poppa" Guttmann labelled Friendship, Unity and Sportsmanship. I have my own interpretation: Disability, Ability and Capability. Disability are the bits that don't work, Ability are the bits that do work, and Capability is how you make them work.'

Anyone who breaks his back now and goes to a spinal injuries unit will, as soon as he can, have to put some time in on three sports: archery, table tennis and swimming. Archery builds up the muscles, table tennis helps with balance, and swimming gives freedom from the chair, arm movements and breathing – anyone with a high spinal fracture is going to have some breathing problems. That provides a taste of sport, and if anyone is interested after leaving hospital, he joins a local club and gets on with it as well as he can. The coaching, unfortunately, is more likely to be kind and well-intentioned than expert.

'I don't believe there should be sports clubs for the disabled and sports clubs for the able-bodied, they should be one. Our technique is able-bodied technique, as far as we can use it, but too often we are treated quite differently. We need to be coached by the able-bodied, but they should be coaches from the able-bodied world, not drop-outs from the able-bodied world. That's perhaps a bit rude, but you know what I mean: there's no point in being coached for the discus by someone who was quite good at vaulting over horses in the gym and is kind enough to give up some time to the disabled. This is our great problem: we're getting people to coach us who would never have thought about being coaches in the able-bodied world – or who would never have been accepted as coaches there.

'We have to be grateful, I know that, because that's what we're supposed to be, because after all we're only the disabled. But sport for the disabled now shouldn't be such a surprise, such a secondary thought – it's been going on publicly for thirty-six years. If you're advertising for a

Carefree days for Margaret with Father Christmas, a tin bath and her happy teens.
(*Ivy Hough*)

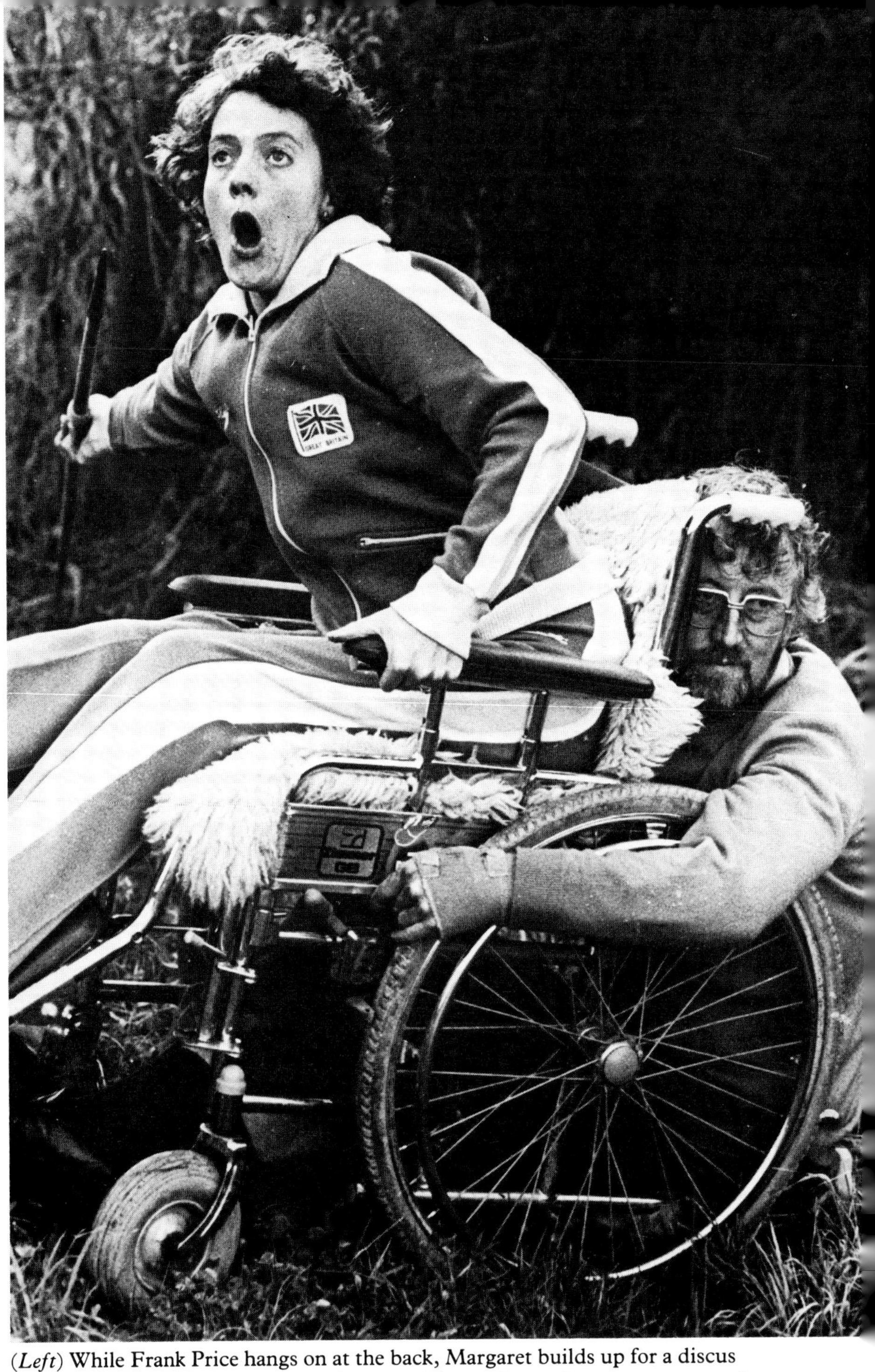

(*Left*) While Frank Price hangs on at the back, Margaret builds up for a discus throw . . . and (*above*) gives the javelin everything she's got. It was never enough. (*Eamonn McCabe*)

Shot putting is not a matter to be taken lightly: even hers weighed $6\frac{1}{2}$ pounds. (*Eamonn McCabe*)

If you don't shout when you put the shot, she said, you don't get a good explosion.
(*Eamonn McCabe*)

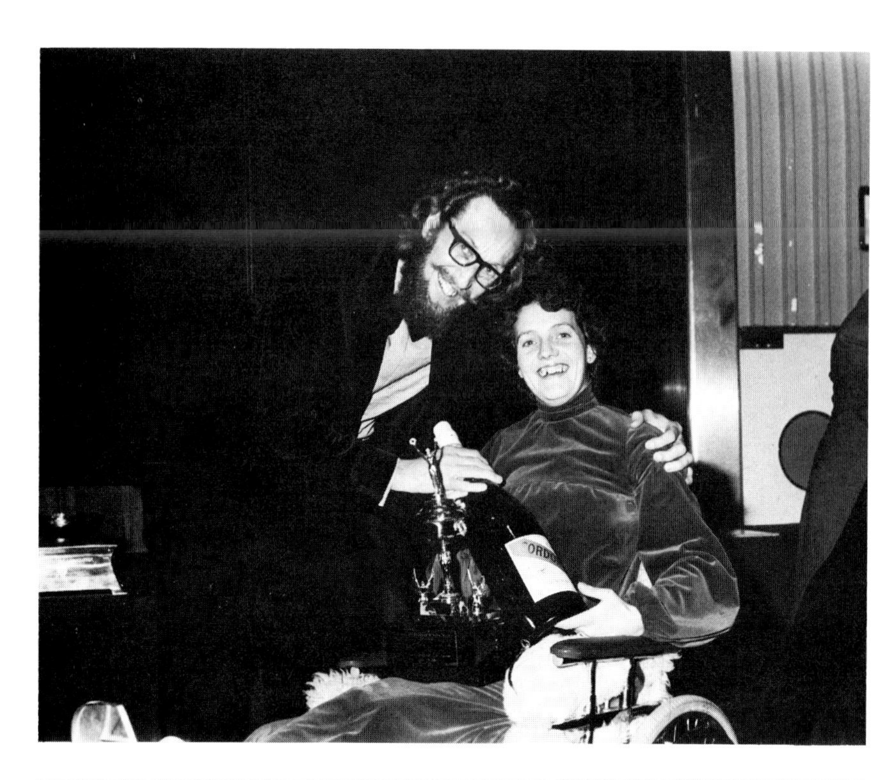

Receiving the Sports Writers' Association's McGowran Trophy in 1979, with the author (*top*), and in 1980, with middleweight champion Alan Minter. (*Derek Rowe*)

Two more moments to remember: *This Is Your Life*, 1981, with David Wilkie looking on, (*Sports Council*), and 'You are my wife', 1978. (*Kent Photos*)

At the gates of Buckingham Palace: Frank, Margaret and the treasured MBE. (*Maurice Carroll*)

manager for the British paraplegic sports team (and they seldom do), you'd be far better to get someone who knows something about sports management, like an out-of-work football manager, than a very nice retired bank manager who knows nothing about sport. Well, wouldn't you?'

Margaret is magnificent when she is in full flow. Discretion and diplomacy may not be among her bedfellows, and there are times when she is reluctant to consider the other point of view; but the certainty of her conviction and the honesty of her argument are as compelling as the spirit with which she puts them over. She leaves behind her a trail of tender toes, but she sweeps on towards targets that need to be struck. She was stunned to meet at the National Games once a girl ten years younger than she was, and of Margaret's class of disability, who had dropped out of sport when Margaret came in because she knew she wouldn't stand a chance.

'She said to me, "When I did it, it was all a bit of fun. You take it too serious. It used to be a bit of a giggle, but not since you came in." I told her to turn round and look at the stadium: "Do you think that was built for a giggle, because I don't." There's nothing wrong with using sport as a means of meeting friends and enjoying yourself, but what's that kind of person doing at the national championships?'

It's a good thing that Margaret did not overhear a member of the British paraplegic team at the Arnhem Olympics for the Disabled. A man of mature years, much respected in the game, he saw Margaret break another world record and wheeled himself off, shaking his head: 'That's not what it's about,' he said, 'that's not what it's about.' He was giving voice to the feeling within the movement that it was somehow unfair of Margaret to do so much and to do it so well. 'I know,' she said, 'that certain people in the British team thought I took it too seriously and trained too hard. But I could never see why you shouldn't be allowed to, if you're prepared to take the hard training and the mental pressure that goes with being the best in the world.'

As long as the pressures of training remain a pleasure, the mental strain of competition is tolerable, and it was so with Margaret to the end. The fact that she was training for two entirely different areas of activity gave her greater rather than less pleasure, with its constant variety of exercise. This was proved in the most conclusive manner during the year leading up to the 1980 Olympics, when she was warned that it might be a question of competing either in the water or on the field at Arnhem. Since swimming was her natural event, she dropped her field events training and devoted her time to the pool; and her swimming standard began to go down.

'I struggled through my training, didn't enjoy it as much, and couldn't bring out of myself what I knew I had. When we wanted to record a good time I tried hard enough, but I didn't get anywhere. The whole thing was beginning to be very, very hard.

'So we thought perhaps I'd overdone the swimming. We dropped it for a bit, and just concentrated on field events. But there was something lacking. I'd get out in the garden and go to throw and I couldn't get it right. I felt niggly, kept finding fault with the chair or my position or something; I just didn't seem able to get it all together at the same time. So we decided to go for both and let someone else decide which to pick me for. I never looked back, and after the nationals they had to pick me for the lot. Someone else might have been able to give up one side and excel in the other, but I couldn't. Instead of giving me something extra, it seemed to take something out of me.'

It used to be weird to walk down that deserted little Devonshire lane and see, briefly, a discus in flight above a scruffy hedge. If you peered through, you would see this extraordinary sight, this unbelievable sight, of a tracksuited woman in a wheelchair, gripping its arm with her left hand. Almost lost behind it and under it, this grizzle-bearded, bespectacled little man, hanging on as if to stop the chair being blasted into orbit. In her right hand, the discus, a thing about as big as a pudding plate. Her head is turned to the left, her eyes fixed high on an invisible target; her right arm extended diagonally down and slightly behind her. Once, twice, with measured precision, the gripping hand is brought close to the face, the arm bending only from the elbow. Then the breathing changes gear, the stretch is longer, the face contorts in an ecstasy of effort and the swing of the arm lifts the right shoulder sharply away from the back of the chair. The roses rustle in consternation nearly fifty feet away and Frank patters off to retrieve.

The discus is one of the Olympic originals, or to be more accurate one of the very early events of the ancient Olympic Games, contested in 708 BC. It is made of wood with metal plates set flush into the sides, tapering from its thickest point at the centre to the rim - rather in the way that two pudding plates would if you put them face to face. It is surprisingly heavy: two kilos for a man and one for a woman (about 2 lb 3 oz), and is held flat against the hand with the fingers curled round the rim. It can be released off the middle finger (as Margaret did) or the forefinger, and the secret of maximum flight is to release it flat, spinning fast without wobble. Margaret's minutely careful technique was probably as near perfection as it could be, though as she frequently points out, it should only be used as a basis on which the individual needs to impose the adaptations that suit his own abilities best.

'When I'm teaching discus, I like to see people straight away put the chair in the position they think will be best and then get on and throw it. Once you've seen them throw, you can start working back, working out what movements they have and how they should use them to the full. Then I want them to get the feel of the discus, to play with it and handle it with confidence. If you hold it with a straight arm down the side of the chair, swing it backwards and forwards and release it as if you were playing bowls, it should roll in a straight line – and that's one of the most important things to learn about discus throwing. You've got to have a flat hand and a straight, flat thumb. When you've got the hang of that, toss the discus about a bit. Spin it, chuck it up in the air and catch it, feel its shape, get really familiar with it.

'Now let's get the chair right. An able-bodied thrower knows where he wants his feet to be at the end of his spin, and for just the same reason the chair has got to be in the best position for you to get the maximum distance. I know that my front wheels have to be turned backwards, and a line between the centre of the casters has to be parallel with the line of throw. That was my position of maximum result, but it wouldn't be the same for everyone. For instance, I can't get as much turn as some because of my body jacket, and I've always had to work within that restriction. People with balance can sit forward, away from the back of the chair, and use the trunk to rotate. I can't. My left shoulder, the left side of my upper back, is always pressed against the back of the chair. Once that's gone, I'm off balance. When I release, it looks as though my trunk is rotating, but it's not, because there's no rotation there. I'm just pulling across as hard as I can, lifting one shoulder forward and pressing the other back.

'If you watch discus throwers, you see them swing once, swing twice, swing three times with the full arm. I started off using a couple of swings, but I realised it was wasting my strength. By the time I was smashing world records, I'd done away with all swings. People with proper left arm use, which I don't have, can point up with that hand to get the direction right. It's very important to look high and aim high, to look to the apex of its flight, even if you do have to hold on to the arm of the chair with your left hand as I did. Some people when they do their swinging use the left hand to hold the discus upright, or actually turn the right hand over so the discus doesn't drop out. I found that swinging was dividing my concentration: my brain was having to think, don't drop the discus, keep your balance, don't slump, keep your hand flat. When I'd sorted myself out I found the best thing, for me, was to hold on to the chair with my left hand from the beginning, feel the discus, get the balance, "bounce it" twice with my arm bending from the elbow, take it right back and throw. The power comes from the shoulder and upper arm, your thumb guides it, your wrist flicks it, your fingers release it. It should come out flat and spinning.'

In the finals of the International Stoke Mandeville Games of 1981, Margaret broke the world record with each of her three throws. Each one was perfectly flat. In the build-up to the Games, she had been spending between two and four hours at practice *every day*.

There was never any chance that Margaret could throw the javelin well, and it was surprising that she persisted with it. Her cervical disability prevented her from reaching back and throwing forward, so she had to throw across her chest in a movement that was remarkably elegant but inevitably inefficient. Thus she never got to be the best in the world, only the second best (in 1981); but she was, of course, the national champion. In the able-bodied, this discipline produces some of the most graceful and exciting competitors, with its nice balance of speed, strength, timing and perfect co-ordination. A woman's javelin weighs 600 grams (1 lb 5 oz), is 7 ft 6 in long and will now travel, at best, about 75 metres (246 ft) – though twenty-five years ago the women's world record was only 188 feet.

Without the momentum engendered by the thirty-metre sprint that normally precedes its release, paraplegics are a very long way behind figures like that, but nevertheless have covered impressive distances. An able-bodied thrower, at the end of his run, side-steps so that for a moment it looks as if the release will be across the chest; but the step that follows is vital. It brings him square to the line at the instant of release, the arm coming from low behind him in a whiplash movement not unlike that used for throwing a cricket ball (it has been suggested that the outstanding success of the Finnish nation at this sport is due to their life-long experience of throwing snowballs!).

Those girls in Margaret's disability class who could push their bodies forward a little and bring the javelin even from shoulder level were generally the best throwers. 'I learned not to expect too much,' said Margaret – so a silver medal in the International Games and a bronze in the Olympics cannot have been too disappointing. Because she has no experience of the right way to throw a javelin, she is reluctant to attempt to coach it: 'I can teach children the basics, and I might get them up to international standard, but I can't finish them off. To put the final touches, you've got to have done it yourself. That's why we need able-bodied coaches. The trouble is, as we've said before, that the usual able-bodied person who is teaching sport to disabled children is doing it just to involve them in something, which is fine; but generally he doesn't know enough about the subject in detail to be able to maximise their potential. He doesn't know what the whistle of the fingers or the flick of the wrist means.'

Substitute a spear for a javelin, and you can see that the origins of that event go back pretty far into man's history. The shot put has even more martial beginnings, but not quite such distant ones: throwing cannon balls, from the fourteenth century onwards. It always looks an ungainly activity, practised by mountainous athletes. An able-bodied man's shot weighs 16 lb and a woman's nearly 9 lb (4 kilos), but the shot used by Margaret's class was 3 kilos, three times the weight of her discus. It is cupped not in the palm, but at the base of the fingers, and nestles in the hollow of the neck during the preparatory movements. As with the discus, throwers work from within a circle, out of which they must not step until the implement has come to rest. The distance of the throw is measured from the point of landing to the circumference of the throwing circle, so it is vital for both able-bodied and disabled throwers to release from as near the edge as possible.

'I know it looks a very muscular event,' said Margaret, 'but technique is very important - and particularly for us, because obviously we haven't got the strength you really need to shift that thing. It feels very heavy and you have to take care: if a paraplegic drops a shot on her legs, it can do a lot of damage. In the same way that cuts and sores don't heal easily on a paralysed area, so bruises often don't come up to the surface like they do with you. They go down and spread inside. So you have to get children to respect the shot very seriously.

'To get an idea of their potential, we get them to hold the shot in front of them, palm up and fingers forward, and throw it up and back over their shoulder. When I was competing, as a loosener I used to put it up in the air and catch it again a few times, with one hand. While we're on that, you can't stress too much the importance of warming up properly. Your body has got to be loose and warm before you stretch it violently, otherwise you're sure to damage a muscle. When an able-bodied athlete does that it's bad luck, a mishap; when it happens to one of us, you'll always get the cynic who says there you are, I said they shouldn't be doing it.

'You must get the technique right for the shot, or you'll get nowhere. It mustn't come away from your neck until you're about to project it, and when it does come away, it must only be on a forward movement. If you lead with your elbow, which you will do if you move the shot backwards from your neck, it's a no-throw. Get those things right first, and get your chair in the right position, and you can worry later about how far you might be able to put it.

'It's a highly explosive event, shot-putting, especially with the disabled. From nothing, with no movement, you suddenly have to release all that strength in the right direction. You have to explode, yourself, you really do. It's very difficult to get people to shout when they put, but that's what you need. They know that when they swim, they've got to breathe properly, but in the field events they don't think about it. You must get your breathing under control first, with a few deep breaths. Then when it comes to that moment of release, you really expel, you shout. Same as Jimmy Connors when he's serving. He's exploding. It doesn't matter if some people don't think it's very nice; when you're competing, you're out to do the very best you can, win or lose. If you don't make a noise, or you worry about people hearing you, then you're not going to compete to the best of your ability.'

During that summer of '79 she showed what was meant by 'the best of your ability'. In the International Games she whitewashed the world, collecting gold medals in the shot, discus and all six of her swimming events – 50 metres breaststroke, backstroke and freestyle, the 3 × 25 metres individual medley, the 3 × 50 team medley relay and the 4 × 50 team freestyle relay, in which Britain lowered the world record by no less than eighteen seconds. She also, in that one meeting at the end of July, set new world records in the shot and discus, and retained her backstroke record from the previous year, and the freestyle record that she had set a few weeks earlier – when she lowered her own mark by nearly five seconds.

She was beginning to look outrageously good, and at last someone cared. At the end of November a telegram reached the cottage which read: 'PLEASE PHONE SOONEST HUNN OF THE OBSERVER.' She hadn't a clue what it might be about, but he broke the news to her that she had won the Bill McGowran Trophy as the Disabled Sports Personality of the Year, to be presented in December at the annual awards dinner of the Sports Writers' Association of Great Britain. The writer and the newspaper's award-winning sports photographer, Eamonn McCabe, took the train to Exeter and there hired a car to head for unknown territory - not without difficulty, since one of them had lost his driving licence and the other had left his at home.

It was one of those jobs you don't forget. Eamonn McCabe's picture of Margaret throwing the discus in her garden, with Frank the gnome buried behind the chair, was seen around the world and is now on the jacket of this book. *The Observer* published it at the end of the week in which she won the SWA's award, and on the strength of that named her their own Sports Personality of the Week, which brought her a jeroboam of Mumm champagne. It is fairly clear that the writer had had an experience denied to most sports writers: 'A guy could get pretty angry after sharing a day with Margaret Price,' he concluded. 'You want to kill the man who drove the Mini that didn't stop at a zebra crossing in Folkestone. You want to weep at the meanness of society's support for the impossibly afflicted, and wonder why sports sponsorship is reserved for the able-bodied.

'Above all, you can't help wanting to say what a waste, what a tragedy that this bright life should have been ruined. How wrong that would be: the tragedy is there, of course, but this marvellous woman is no ruin. The body is imprisoned on its sheepskin rug, but a new life burns within it, brighter than most of ours. It has twice our determination, twice our love, twice our happiness - and, for shame, let us not begin to measure our achievements against those of Margaret Price.'

10 Olympic Glory

If you are going to dismiss sport for the disabled because the results are pathetic in comparison with those of the able-bodied, you may have started on a principle of exclusion of which you can hardly see the finish. You would, presumably, wipe out the Boys' Club boxing finals (one of the great sporting nights of the year), any Extra 'B' XV rugby match and women's tennis right through to Lloyd and Navratilova. You would cease to be interested in soccer in Divisions II, III and IV, even though all their players are putting maximum effort into a contest of skill and athleticism - which is just what the disabled do.

There are times when disabled events are embarrassingly feeble, and if only we could lose the sense of pity that we feel for the handicapped, we would be able to give them the bird just as we do the able-bodied: 'What a load of rubbish!' would ring out over Stoke Mandeville Stadium and we would blow raspberries when a one-legged high jumper knocked the bar off at five feet.

Now, you're having me on! A one-legged high jumper? Yes indeed. For though Ludwig Guttmann and Stoke Mandeville were concerned only with spinal injuries, and though the annual national and international games there are only for paraplegics, other categories of physical (and mental) disability hold their own sports meetings, and many of them meet in the World or the Olympic Games for the Disabled. At Arnhem in 1980 the wheelchair athletes were joined by the blind, the amputees and the cerebral palsied, and a greater feast of desperate effort it would be hard to find. Alone among the British Press, as they often are, *The Observer* sent a reporter to Arnhem. His article, written midway through the two weeks of competition, is worth reading if only for the fact that it represents an instant reaction from an open mind, neither prejudged nor given the benefit of subsequent lengthy consideration:

'You might think that to have watched a man with one leg playing table tennis against a man with one arm was to have seen it all. You would be wrong. Two tables along a man with one leg and no hands was playing a man with no arms. Sympathy seemed singularly inappropriate, since they played better than anyone likely to live within a mile of most of us.

The anatomical details cannot be escaped. One held the bat in a shoulder-high, thalidomidic flipper; the other had it firmly pincered between two stumps, one above and one below the elbow. At service time, the ball popped neatly out of his mouth. Let us never again use the word "impossible".

This festival of sport from which defeat has been eliminated is called the Olympic Games for the Disabled. That is a cold word, disabled, and not one to which the competitors subscribe. Handicapped they know they are, and in the beautiful Dutch National Sports Centre at Arnhem, handicaps they are overcoming.

If the public know anything about this quadrennial battle, they know it as the "wheelchair Olympics". That is no longer accurate. In Toronto four years ago, amputees and the blind were admitted as well as paraplegics, and in Arnhem they have been joined by the cerebral palsied (spastics).

As these four categories of the handicapped are each divided into groups according to the extent of the handicap (there are eight groups of the paralysed and nine of amputees) and each has its own programme of events, the overall picture to the spectator is often confusing and sometimes positively tiresome.

In terms of sporting standards, the performances range from the superb to the agonising; from Britain's Margaret Price, for instance, to the Polish woman who, alone, ran one lap of the track on two artificial legs and took seven and a half minutes to do so. Gold is good, they say, but to compete is victory. The joyous Mrs Price, a thirty-year-old Devonian paralysed up to her armpits, opened her account on Monday night by winning the three-stroke individual swimming medley half a length of the pool ahead of all rivals.

This week she goes for three individual golds, but so far the sensation of the Games has been another British swimmer, 35-year-old Mike Kenny. Kenny is a Class 1a tetraplegic, the possessor of a body so helpless that cutting the meat on his plate is often beyond him. Thanks to his blessed buoyancy in the water, he won in two days gold medals in the 25 metres freestyle, breaststroke and backstroke, failing only in the last to break the world and Olympic records he already held.

You only need spend two days at Arnhem to want to hand out champagne to all 110 British competitors, all 2,000 of the athletes from 43 nations who smile and struggle there. Sympathy moves you, then admiration drives you, but pretty soon you are involved in the sheer joy of the combat and of the international camaraderie that surrounds it. To hell with politics, this is sport, and the dearest wish of the participants is not for the sympathy of the able-bodied, but for the attention of the other ninety per cent of the disabled. It is a major tragedy for their rehabilitation that most of the handicapped don't realise the possibilities in sport. Far fewer would ever have tasted them but for the determination of Sir

Ludwig Guttmann, who died in March more than thirty years after initiating the first Paraplegic Games at Stoke Mandeville.

The media usually steer clear of them, thinking their public would count them distasteful. But the faint surprise of finding yourself surrounded by flashing stumps soon passes and the swimming pool becomes a concerto of lost limbs. One-legged men cast off their encumbrances and hop hugely over the high jump, the blind dash down the dark tunnel of the sprinting track, and in the basketball hall the knives are out.

Wheelchairs hurtle from end to end, mighty shoulders heave and jostle, and the obstructing is something shocking. Every now and then a major collision overturns a chair and out flies a body. The top is all muscle, the legs only rags. They don't expect help and they seldom get it.

Out in the athletics stadium it's raining again, but they press on with the medal ceremonies. A vast American shot putter, blind, has just added twenty-nine inches to the world record. He turns to feel for the man on the podium below him. They meet, clutch, embrace. The third man finds his way in and now six arms are hugging in a bundle of love and tears and triumph. It's much the same in the grandstand, but we're a bit short on triumph.'

To sharpen the accuracy, there were in fact not 2,000 athletes from 43 nations, but 1,968 from 42. The Dutch government decided to oppose the admission of the team from South Africa. There were 855 paraplegics, 447 amputees, 341 blind and 125 cerebral palsied, and they came with a total of 420 escorts. The host nation's turnout of 143 competitors was exceeded by 150 from the United States and 155 from West Germany; at the other end of the scale were 5 paraplegics from Zimbabwe, 4 from the

Bahamas and 1 from Ethiopia. There were some puzzling statistics among them: though France brought 26 cerebral palsied, they had only 2 blind competitors; Germany, with 35 blind, entered 1 with cerebral palsy; Yugoslavia came with only 10 paraplegics, but 20 amputees. The United Kingdom's total entry of 109 comprised 59 paraplegics, 22 amputees, 22 blind and 6 cerebral palsied; between them they won 46 gold medals, 33 silver and 22 bronze of the 2,300 on offer.

The organisation required to cope with a meeting of this size (there were far more competitors than had attended the able-bodied Olympics in Los Angeles less than fifty years earlier) was no part-time affair – though the running of it depended on hundreds of volunteers. The Director-General and the Sports Director were working on it for twenty months; by the end of 1978, eighteen months before the opening, there were five full-time workers, and by the beginning of 1980 there were twenty. When recruiting of part-timers was complete for the opening in June, nearly 2,500 people were working at or between the various centres of the Games and the budget of 15 million guilder (about £3.3 million) was beginning to dribble away.

Nine of the twelve sports of the Games took place at the National Sports Centre at Papendal, near Arnhem: fencing, weight-lifting, goal ball (a game for the blind in which teams of three try to roll a ball with a bell in it past their opponents), table tennis, wrestling (for the blind), shooting, archery, bowls and athletics. Basketball and volleyball took place in the largest sports hall in the Netherlands, the Rijnhal, on the banks of the Rhine, and the swimming was in a magnificent 50-metre pool at Veenendaal. Six miles from Papendal was the temporary Olympic Village, an army camp which had been given over to the athletes and their escorts under an unusual burgomaster, Lady Sabine de Jonge van Ellemeet.

With more than a thousand wheelchair competitors,

transport arrangements were unusually complicated. How do you wheel yourself on to a bus? First, you spend £67,000 adapting fifty single-deck buses so that they can accommodate fourteen wheelchairs and nineteen other passengers - and each wheelchair is clamped securely to the floor. Then you build long wooden ramps at every alighting point - ten of them in the Village alone - that take the chairs to the exact level of the bus floor. So many of the Dutch public transport companies wanted to supply coaches that they had to draw lots for the privilege, and to find the 150 drivers necessary was no problem at all. In case of any trouble with traffic jams, the buses had red, white and blue markings on the sides and the roof, so that police on the ground and in the air could easily find them.

They are not likely to believe it in Britain, but there were 120 representatives of the Press and broadcasting media from around the world, who found a perfectly equipped Press Centre with telephones, telex, typewriters, television and a power supply for every desk; and a bar. There was also a daily paper, the Olympic Village Daily, known as the smallest international newspaper with the shortest life. It was a four-page freebie that covered the events of the previous day, with full results, and published the programme of the current day, the menu in the Village restaurant and other scraps of information.

It was to this marvellously conceived, if somewhat inflexible organisation that the British team arrived from Stansted Airport on the Tuesday before the Olympics opened. There was no lack of excitement or of determination, though Margaret felt that as usual there had been insufficient attention to team training. Getting paraplegics into an aeroplane is quite a business. Every one of the fifty-nine had to be transferred to a temporary wheelchair while their own were loaded, and in these comparatively unstable chairs they had to be put on the lift that normally takes supplies to the galley door. In the Village at Arnhem,

they slept ten to a dormitory and Margaret's lot were lucky enough to have with them the British nurse, an escort and one able-bodied coach. There were three days in which to settle down and get into peak condition before the Games opened.

'As usual, we didn't make the best use of them. The British attitude seemed to be, "Well, you're here, and if you're not good enough to win now, you never will be." I knew my own training would see me through, but if there had been a greater effort and a more organised approach by the management, we might have done better as a team.

They just don't have the competitive drive that I would like to see. It was the Olympic Games, after all.'

The opening ceremony was as memorable as most of the able-bodied kind and seemed to capture the essence of the occasion: 'I was proud enough to have been chosen for my country in the first place, but when you sat there in your uniform, with all the athletes from all over the world, I can't tell you what it felt like. It was a beautiful experience and I shall never forget it.'

Frank had not been allowed to accompany Margaret to Holland, nor could he be with her during competition, but he and her family had come over by car and rented a chalet some miles away. They were there for the ceremony, right beside the ramp down which the paraplegic athletes were wheeled. The amputees, the blind and the cerebral palsied competitors and their escorts were already in the stand when the chairs were pushed round the track and into the middle of the arena. As she came down the ramp, Margaret saw Frank for the first time since she had left England: 'It was a very emotional experience – for them as well, I think most of them were crying. For me, it was the proudest moment of my life.'

Over the next eleven days, it was hard to keep pride down. In the nine events for which she was entered, Margaret won five gold medals, two silver and two bronze. In three days of the second week she won four gold medals and set four world records – one of them in the heat of an event in which she eventually finished second. Such a plethora of success comes close to being embarrassing. It will for ever remain one of the most amazing performances in the history of sport for the disabled – the more so because of an injury she sustained after completing only three of the nine events. Let us consider dispassionately those days at Arnhem.

Monday: the three-stroke individual swimming medley, back, breast and freestyle, 25 metres each leg. Swum without heats, straight into the final. Margaret wins by a ludicrous margin, but not in as fast a time as that which she set earlier in the summer for a world record at Stoke Mandeville. 'No problems, but I could have done better if that final had not been my very first Olympic event. Our coach said I shouldn't be nervous because I had done this sort of thing before, which just shows how much they know about it. The coaches don't seem to believe in pre-swim thoughts, but I like to sit very quietly and prepare for the event. They reckoned I wasn't a good sport because I wouldn't sit and cheer for the others, but there's no way I could do that immediately before a swim. Afterwards, yes, but not before. They just have no understanding of it at all.'

Tuesday: no competition for Margaret.

Wednesday: three-stroke team medley relay, 50 metres each leg. Margaret opens, with the backstroke. In this event, each team can only have one swimmer from Class 4 and one from Class 3 in their three, but it doesn't matter in which order you swim them. Britain finished with the silver medal: 'We broke the old world record, but Poland broke it better.'

Thursday: javelin. You get three throws in the preliminaries, and then the six highest have another three. Moving into the final, Margaret is in fourth place: 'It's always been my worst event. I broke the British record, yes, but that doesn't mean a lot. But I knew I had something more to give, so in the final I really put an effort in. That's when my hand went. I nearly fell out of the chair and grabbed the right arm to stop myself, which didn't help.'

She got the bronze medal, but at the expense of apparently torn ligaments at the base of her right thumb. (When, months later, the injury had still not healed, a broken bone was discovered.) With six more events to go, can she stand it? The British team doctor, a Stoke Mandeville man, examines the hand and actually asks Margaret if she wants an x-ray. Fearing what it might disclose, and that she would be stopped from competing, she says she doesn't. The word gets back to the British team manager that she refuses to be x-rayed, and he says it must be done or she will be banned from the rest of the Games.

The nurse takes her off to the Dutch doctor in their sporting injuries unit, a man very sympathetic to her urge to go on competing, but a doctor who must protect the patient. He looks at the note from the British doctor: '*Left* hand to be x-rayed.' Margaret's eyes grow wide as saucers, she whips off her wedding ring and the left hand is x-rayed. Then the Dutchman straps up her right hand and makes her promise that Frank will bring her in for treatment every day and he will review the situation. Because she must not compete with strapping on, he gives her plenty of spare strapping with which to replace it. By great good fortune, there are four days before she has to compete again.

Tuesday: a heavy day, shot in the morning, breaststroke and team freestyle relay in the evening. Though Frank and family have tickets for the swimming, the place is full when they arrive, sold out. Despite the thumb, it's not a bad day: a gold in the shot, retaining her 1979 world record; a bronze in the 50 metres breaststroke; a gold and a world record for the team in the 4 × 50 metres freestyle relay. The thumb hurts, but it still works.

Wednesday: the discus, the event for which Margaret has honed herself close to perfection. In the previous two International Games at Stoke Mandeville, she has won the gold medals and in 1979 she broke the world record. At Arnhem, she exceeds that mark by more than two feet, but loses the gold and the record to someone who goes a foot further than that (in 1981 she had her revenge, and how!).

Thursday: individual swimming again, 50 metres backstroke and 50 metres freestyle. Gold medals in each, and because they were swum in a long-course pool (50 metres long), they are world records to add to those she already holds for the same events in a short-course pool (25 metres).

For much of the fortnight in Arnhem it had rained, and the weather was so bad for the closing ceremony that the display parachutists were unable to drop. The Minister for Sport, then Mr Hector Munro, sent a message to the team before they left: '... delighted to hear of the tremendous success ... tribute to the dedication and hard work ... In Britain we are proud of you.' Those who ever heard of the team's achievement were proud, but would you need more than two hands to count them? One national paper was going to meet them, but mistook Gatwick for Stansted. Another phoned Margaret's mother and asked if her daughter was, well, you know, suitable for a photograph. There was no national reception, no party to celebrate their glory. Prime Ministers have frequently held parties for less glorious sporting achievements, but this lot were, well, you know, disabled.

11 Honours Galore

Margaret's performance in the Arnhem Olympics of 1980 did not allow the Sports Writers' Association much option but to name her again the Disabled Sports Personality of the Year - a unique honour, for not only had no other athlete won the award in successive years before, but it had never been won twice by the same person. It is puzzling to Margaret and to the rest of us that the management at Stoke Mandeville never seem to have made the use of this award that they might. The award is always made in consultation with them, and in his time Sir Ludwig Guttmann always attended the dinner at which the presentation was made, but if you go to the sports stadium there you will find no mention of it. You would think it would be both interesting and encouraging to young and newly-disabled athletes if they could see some evidence of the honour that the national sports writers annually pay them, but so quiet is the matter kept that in 1979 (the seventeenth occasion on which the great trophy had been presented) Margaret Price herself was unaware of its existence.

'It was news to me. I'd never heard of it, and it wasn't until I saw that list of names on the trophy that I realised it had been going on so long.' The occasion of its presentation is one of sport's social events of the year, a dinner and dance at a major London hotel which is attended by many of the nation's most successful and most respected sports personalities. For thirty-five years the SWA have held the event, at which the most celebrated awards are those to the Sportsman and the Sportswoman of the Year. Unlike the public polls conducted by the BBC and others to make similar nominations, the SWA awards are decided by the Association's membership. The voting is therefore less influenced by personality and public exposure than by actual achievement: indeed the members' brief is that the awards should go to those who have done most to enhance Britain's sporting prestige internationally.

In Margaret's first year the winners of the major awards were Sebastian Coe (who had broken three world track records in forty-one days) and Caroline Bradley, the world's leading female show jumping rider, who so tragically died in 1983. They were not the only award winners of the night: Nottingham Forest Football Club were represented, European Cup winners, as the team of the year; the great former athlete Mary Peters won the J.L. Manning Award, for services to sport outside competition; the bowls maestro David Bryant received the SWA Award for outstanding achievement in sport; and Terry Griffiths, the Welsh postman who become world snooker champion, won the award as International Newcomer of the Year.

Margaret didn't quite know what to expect when she and Frank were invited to the dinner that first year, but it was, she said later, 'Absolutely marvellous! It wasn't just the honour of getting the award from Hector Munro, who was Minister for Sport then, but the excitement of being with all those other athletes. I think it was the first time I really felt like an athlete, not just a disabled athlete. Everybody there was in sport, or had been, or wrote about sport or had sport in their heart, and I'd never been in that sort of company before.'

Hotels may not always be easy for the Prices to cope with, but they never let that stop them accepting an invitation. They get in and sort it out from there. It is not often possible, for example, to get the wheelchair into the bath-

room in a hotel room: 'But that's not so terrible. Obviously if it were your own house, you'd alter it, but for a night it's hardly worth thinking about.' Because of the peculiarities of her liver, there are some foods that Margaret cannot take – fried food, fats, milk, potatoes, and not much pastry, bread or fish. When she knows she's going out for a meal, she takes special care of her diet for two or three days before and after, and on the night it is usually no more of a problem than it is for anyone else on a diet.

The first year of the SWA awards, Margaret wore the red velvet dress she had made for her wedding. In 1980, she wanted to make another one, but the injury to her hand in Arnhem meant it was impossible for her to sew. So, she went shopping: 'It takes me a long time, but it's fun. I've got very firm ideas about what I like and what I don't like, and with my body jacket you can't have anything with a low neckline, or something tight fitting.' Frank wheeled her around the Bromley shops, where her mother lives, for a day or two. Trying dresses on, particularly long ones, is no joke – though Margaret always turns it into one. Frank has to go in with her, and the changing cubicles are so small it's often worse, she says, than trying to go to the loo. When they finally found the dress she wanted, the assistant let them use the staff room for fitting it. It was a lightweight item of pale yellow chiffon with orange and brown flowers, and as usual she looked terrific. Her vitality and enthusiasm, even from the confines of a wheelchair, are more remarkable in public than they are in private, contrasting as they do with the restrained politeness displayed by the average guest at a formal party.

Sebastian Coe was again the Sportsman of the Year, this time for his gold and silver medals in Moscow, and he followed Tony Jacklin's achievement of a decade earlier in winning the award in two successive years. Sportswoman was Margaret's swimming companion from Kelly College, Sharron Davies. Margaret's trophy was presented this time by Alan Minter, the former world middleweight boxing champion. Seeing that she had her hand in plaster, Minter shook it delicately; when he shook her husband's hand, Frank thought he was never going to get it back in one piece.

There was another guest at that dinner with whom Margaret had a special link that neither of them realised at the time: the Kent and England bowler, 'Deadly' Derek Underwood. Their connection was a letter, two presumably identical letters posted by the same hand on the same day in mid-November. The postman came to the Prices' cottage at about half-past seven in the morning, while madam was still in bed. Frank went to pick it up and as he saw it on the mat he called out, 'Margaret, you've got your call-up papers.' Printed across the top of the long white envelope was 'On Her Majesty's Service', but as he carried it back to Margaret he saw in smaller type in the bottom left-hand corner the words 'Prime Minister'.

'What's she after?' he said. As usual, Margaret hadn't a clue, and thought someone up there was rounding up opinions on facilities for disabled sport, or something of that kind. Margaret opened it, scanned it and could hardly believe it. 'Here, Frank,' she called. 'Read this!'

'Urgent', it also said on the envelope, and 'Personal'. On the letter, under the heading '10 Downing Street' (no town, no postal code), were the words 'From the Principal Private Secretary - IN CONFIDENCE.'

> 'Madam, The Prime Minister has asked me to inform you, in strict confidence, that she has it in mind, on the occasion of the forthcoming list of New Year Honours, to submit your name to The Queen with a recommendation that Her Majesty may be graciously pleased to approve that you be appointed a Member of the Order of the British Empire.
>
> Before doing so, the Prime Minister would be glad to be assured that this would be agreeable to you. I should be grateful if you would let me know by completing the enclosed form and sending it to me by return of post.'

And Mr V.A. Whitmore assured Mrs M.A. Price that he was, Madam, her obedient Servant. Few of those who receive that letter ever actually expect it, and for Margaret the thrill was indescribable. Apart from recognising the change in sex of the Prime Minister, the wording of the letter appears not to have changed for years and its impact has certainly not lessened. The form of acceptance went back pronto (what would have happened had they been on one of their three-week visits to Bromley?) and they steeled themselves not to whisper a word to a soul. 'It was lovely being at home when the news came, because we could shout it to each other and there wasn't a soul who could hear.'

Margaret is pedantically proud of her honour: 'When I sign my name now, it's "Margaret Price, M.B.E." If the Queen has given me an award, I should use it – I feel very strongly about that. As for giving it back, I think that's terrible. You have the chance to refuse it in the first place, when that letter comes. If you don't believe in it, that's the time to do it, not after you've got it.'

After that letter came, it was amazing, they both said, how often the subject of awards and honours seemed to crop up in conversation when they were with other people, and they would shoot a quick glance at each other. They longed to be able to write on the Christmas cards they were sending, 'Look for the New Year's Honours List!', but they never did. They didn't even hint at it to Mrs Hough, though as usual they stayed there through the Christmas season.

With New Year's Day being a Bank Holiday, and without papers, they supposed that the list would be published the next day. But early on the morning of 31 December there was a phone call for Margaret from one of her aunts: 'Congratulations, I'm so happy for you.' 'What did Molly want?' asked Mrs Hough. 'Just thanking us for the Christmas present,' Margaret said. Still they kept it a secret, wanting her mother to read it for herself, and at last Mrs Hough went out as usual to collect her paper. Another call of congratulations came while she was out, and as soon as she came in with the paper (the *Daily Express*) the Prices had a quick look: not a word about it. It became almost unbearable, and Frank sneaked out to find a paper that was carrying the news. He came back and laid it on the table.

'Here, Mum,' he said casually, 'read this.' But Mum was, she said, busy for a minute. No, he said, come on. And she came on and read it and squealed with delight. Not a bad way to end 1980. Not a bad year: five Olympic gold medals, two silver, two bronze; a second successive award as the Disabled Sports Personality of the Year; and an MBE. Whatever it brought, 1981 could scarcely be more dramatic. Or could it?

Towards the end of February Margaret and Frank went up to stay again at Bromley, to be with the parents before they went on a six-month trip to Australia, where daughter Jean was getting married. The London visit fitted in neatly with an invitation to Margaret from the Sports Council to take part in an informal seminar with some able-bodied sportsmen, where they wanted her to discuss the problems experienced by the disabled when they attended events such as Test matches and First Division football. The Sports Council management said that as parking would be difficult around Knightsbridge, where their offices then were, they would send a car to pick up the Prices from Bromley. It turned out to be a slightly mysterious journey with an unexpected end.

Since they were travelling from north Kent to the West End in the evening rush hour, Margaret guided the chauffeur through some of the short cuts south of the Thames. Neither the Prices nor, apparently, the chauffeur knew exactly where the Sports Council offices were, and when they arrived somewhere near the right area they were all alarmed to hear a metallic grinding sound every time the driver put his foot on the brake.

'I've got a problem here,' the driver said. 'Do you know how far it is now?' Not a clue, was the answer, so he stopped and went into a sweet shop to ask them if they knew. 'It's all right,' he said when he emerged, 'it's only just down the road a bit, so we should manage. You watch out for the numbers: we want number 70.' They went past it, did a U-turn in the middle of Knightsbridge, and eventually landed at the right door at the right time.

There were indeed a lot of sportsmen gathered in the offices. Margaret remembers, apart from Dick Jeeps, the Sports Council chairman, such names as David Wilkie,

Sharron Davies, Alan Pascoe, Linsey MacDonald, Wendy Norman, Rachel Flint, Trevor Brooking and Paul Mariner. She was in the midst of them when another familiar face appeared from nowhere and a voice that most people in Britain could identify said, into a microphone: 'Margaret Price, MBE, This Is Your Life.'

'I assume he came through the door,' Margaret said later, 'but for all I knew he came straight up through the floorboards. Even Frank didn't see him coming, and he was expecting him. I took one look at his face and I thought, "It is, it is." I'd seen the television camera in the room, of course, but the Sports Council had told me beforehand that, with it being the Year of the Disabled, Thames TV wanted to cover the discussion.'

If you saw the programme, you may remember that the first sound from Margaret was a rasping sort of gasp. It was one of the rare occasions on which she was not able to control the breathing problems that are always with her. On the other hand Frank, at that moment, was able to turn to Dick Jeeps and whisper: 'I can breathe at last.' It hadn't been easy for him, living with that secret for six weeks during which he was probably not out of her sight for six hours. The closer they came to the day of filming, the more agonising it was – and before the end, of course, other members of the family had to be primed for their part in the deception; some members were even required to deceive each other.

'Because Mum and Dad were going to fly out to Australia the following Tuesday,' Margaret recalled, 'it didn't seem too strange that on the Wednesday evening they said they were going out to see one of the relatives. My brother Colin and his wife Delia, who live in Sidcup, looked in that evening, and I did think it was a bit strange when, soon after Mum had left, Colin said they'd better be getting along. What was in fact happening was that Colin was picking them up in his car and they were all going to the rehearsal, where they have a meal and sit around chatting about the subject (or the victim) and Eamonn Andrews picks up the bits and pieces that he can bring out of them the following night.'

Mr and Mrs Hough were in for a shock at that rehearsal. There they found their daughter Jean and her fiancé, who had been flown in from Australia the previous Sunday to stay in a London hotel, and who had been forbidden to contact the family. During the programme, amid the customary round of emotive sentiment from schoolfriends, nurses, athletes and relations, they included a message from Jean, filmed in front of the Sydney Opera House. That was guaranteed to make even more astonishing the moment when sister Jean's voice was heard off-stage and she was revealed in person.

There have been subjects of *This Is Your Life* who have been so appalled at the prospect that they have walked out as soon as the man with the mike uttered those memorable words. There have been others who have borne the occasion with more stoicism than enjoyment, but Margaret loved every minute of it: 'It's true that you never get someone coming on and saying, "Oh yes, I remember her, a horrible little so-and-so she was," so perhaps it all seems a bit yucky, but then the idea is to produce a really happy evening, and as far as I was concerned they certainly did that.'

If there was a memorable line from the evening it came, as you might expect, from the merry lips of Ivy Hough: 'I always remember the two perfumes she had as a kid – swimming pool and horse manure.' As they walked out of the Sports Council offices, Frank told Eamonn Andrews that they nearly hadn't made it, because they had brake trouble. On the contrary, replied Eamonn, you nearly got here too bloody early.

There were no such stage-managed dramas two weeks later, when they went to Buckingham Palace for Margaret's investiture. With her parents by then in Australia, she took as her two permitted guests Frank and her brother Colin, all well togged up in smart suits, and Margaret with a big felt hat as well and the false tooth she seldom wears to fill the childhood gap. Arriving at Buck House in a wheelchair gives you a special privilege: an entrance at the front, so that you can go up in the lift. Up they went, and then along interminable corridors of china cabinets towards the investiture hall. It had only been two weeks since the engagement of Prince Charles and Lady Diana had been announced, and on their special route the Prices saw both of them – Lady Diana emerging from a room and Prince Charles hurtling down a flight of stairs, until he saw the visitors and proceeded at more princely pace.

'I told Frank and Colin they were to take note of everything they saw, all the decorations, the ceilings and floors, the furniture, the colours – every detail, so that we could tell Mum all about it when she came back. In fact as soon as we got home we did some sketches for her.' The investitures have to be very finely organised. A few days after the honours list has been published you get a letter from the Central Chancery of the Orders of Knighthood at St James's Palace giving you your marching orders (and addressed, of course, to Mrs M.A. Price, MBE):

> 'I am commanded to inform you that an Investiture will be held at Buckingham Palace on Monday, 10th March, 1980, at which your attendance is requested.
>
> I am desired to say that you should arrive at the Palace between the hours of 10 o'clock and 10.30 a.m. and this letter should be shown on entering the gates of the Palace, as no other card of admission is issued to recipients. Cars may be parked in the inner Quadrangle of the Palace under police direction. No windscreen tickets are issued.
>
> If desired, two guests are permitted to accompany

you to watch the Ceremony, and tickets for them may be obtained by making application on the form enclosed herewith which should be returned to me as soon as possible.

The only exception to this rule is that, if a recipient wishes to bring with her her husband and two sons, or two daughters, or a son and daughter, a third ticket will be issued, but in NO circumstances will a fourth ticket be issued.

DRESS

(*a*) Serving Officers and Other Ranks of the Women's Royal Naval Service, Women's Royal Army Corps, Women's Royal Air Force and Members of the Police Force and Fire Brigades should wear the dress laid down in the regulations of their respective Service. Orders, Decorations and Medals should not be worn.
(*b*) Civilians may, if they so desire, wear the uniform of the Civil Organisation or Service to which they belong; otherwise they should wear Day Dress. Orders, Decorations and Medals should not be worn.'

Hats are no longer *de rigueur* for the occasion as they used to be, though they are popular; and there is a trick about gloves of which the wise may advise you: either both on or both off, ladies, but never one of each. After arrival in the area of the investiture the recipients and their guests are swiftly separated (cameras having been confiscated at the entrance), the guests to sit in the body of the hall and the recipients to the anteroom allocated to their particular Order. Margaret's wheelchair brought her special treatment: she was left in an advantageous spot in the investiture hall throughout, so that she had a good view of everything from the knighting downwards: 'The Queen is amazingly graceful with that sword, and it looks enormous.'

When the time comes for the investiture of the Members

of the Order of the British Empire, they queue up in the left-hand corridor of the hall, edging forward at the rate of about one every thirty seconds. The able-bodied are required to take a specified number of paces forward to the Queen, touch Her Majesty's proffered hand (shaking is out), and walk backwards before turning to withdraw. Margaret's chair exempted her from such problems, and her Palace pusher took care of them. Margaret remembers every detail: the Gurkhas and Beefeaters formed the guard behind the Queen, the Scots Guards were playing music in the balcony, the Queen wore turquoise blue but no hat.

The Palace are very firm about who can take photographs and when and where they can do it. Personal cameras are retrieved as the recipients leave the building and may be used in the inner Quadrangle, where a small number of Press and film photographers are allowed and one commercial firm are shooting colour. No other photographers are admitted, so there is usually a good deal of activity of that kind outside the great gates of the forecourt.

That was not Margaret's only visit to the Palace in 1981. Twice in the summer, by extraordinary coincidence, she was there for garden parties: the first time at the invitation of the Lord Lieutenant of Devonshire, and the second when Her Majesty held a garden party for the disabled. On the first occasion it was a brilliant day, on the second it poured. Both times Frank did the job properly in hired topper and tails, a lead followed by few others on the second occasion. Margaret was disgusted at the standard of dress shown by many of the disabled.

'There was a lad there from a school for the disabled at Cheltenham and he was wearing a red sweat-shirt. I ask you, what kind of a headmaster can that be? There was hardly a man dressed properly in the whole party, and some of the behaviour was disgraceful. There were people rushing into the marquees to start eating before the Queen had even got there, and I heard one lot asking if they could take a bag of cakes away because they had a long journey!'

Between the investiture and the garden parties, television screened *This Is Your Life*, as the last programme of that series, and in July came first the national Stoke Mandeville Games and then the International Games. Even by her standards, it was an astonishing summer, not least because of her performances in competition. At the nationals she entered her customary seven individual events, won seven gold medals and set three new world records in swimming: 50 metres freestyle, 50 metres backstroke and 3 × 25 metres individual medley.

At the International Games, in the very last days of July, all her work on the discus over the years reached perfection: the record that had been taken from her in Arnhem with a throw of 16.16 metres was smashed with each one of Margaret's three throws in the final, and she finished with 17.42 metres. Yet again she lowered the world record for the 50 metres freestyle, to a figure that would have seemed impossible only five years earlier: 42.72 seconds. She also took gold medals in the individual medley and the shot, and silvers in the javelin (the best performance of her life) and the 50 metres backstroke and breaststroke. For this stunning achievement, she was for the second time named as *The Observer*'s Sports Personality of the Week. She never competed again.

12 All on Wheels

As the wheels of his chair become the legs and the feet of the paraplegic athlete, it is not surprising that he is every bit as concerned about their style and condition as Steve Cram is about his feet and his running shoes. Those of us who can remember the cumbersome and uncomfortable object that used to be called a bath chair are hardly likely to recognise it as the fore-runner of the type of wheelchair used on the race track at Stoke Mandeville.

Those who race seriously may have spent as much as £1,000 on a custom-built chair - and one that will be of little use to them outside the sports arena. Everything will have been left off it that is not necessary for racing - pushing handles, tipping bars, brakes and side panelling - and what there is will be made of the lightest material providing the necessary strength. The seat and back will not be upholstered, far from it. The back will be as low as the patient can tolerate (dependent largely on the degree of balance he retains) and the seat may have been moulded in fibreglass around his personal posterior. The tyres may remind you of racing bicycles, and can cost up to £70 each, and - particularly for slalom racing - are often set on a camber, the bottoms of the wheels being much further apart than the tops. This gives better manœuvrability through the gates of slalom, and also for the rapid twists and turns of basketball, and in addition provides a zone of greater safety for knuckles, that can be badly scraped by

passing chairs. There are regulations regarding certain of the dimensions – maximum wheel diameter of twenty-six inches, for example, and a statutory height of the seat off the ground of twenty inches – but within the rules there is a wide variation of personal preference. All racing competitors seem to have settled now for the metal rim with which they propel the chair to be about half the diameter of the wheel, and not up near the tyre as it usually is. This makes for far less arm and shoulder movement, which is not only more economical physically, but makes racing possible for some tetraplegics.

Field events competitors like Margaret Price don't need that sort of chair. Strong and solid is the call there, and she has always used the chair in which she lives. That probably accounts for the wigging she gets from the appliance centre at Exeter when she applies for a new one: it's ridiculous, they say, you don't even make yours last for a year. No doubt a mountaineer changes his boots more often than a snooker player.

Her chair costs about £300. She is in it from the moment she leaves her bed to the moment she returns to it. Because of her stiff leg, it is almost impossible to sit in an armchair, and of course her wheelchair has to be provided with a special leg rest; a high back and high sides are necessary because of her lack of balance, and she likes pneumatic casters (the front wheels, at the foot rest) because she and Frank do a lot of 'walking' over fairly rough ground, and solid tyres give her an uncomfortable ride. When her last chair was approaching a state of dilapidation, they went to Exeter to ask for a new one to be ordered. The postman brought it one afternoon and when Frank opened it up it had low arms, a low back, no leg rest and no pneumatic front tyres. That meant another eighty-mile trip to Exeter to take it back and another wait while they sent another one.

'What they seem to be saying,' Margaret said with much disgruntle at the time, 'is that this chair is good enough to sit in at home and you don't have any right to go out. You ask for what you need and they don't listen and give you what they think you ought to want. It's infuriating. This is my life, this chair.'

Its most vital ingredient is the sheepskin rug on which she sits, the material that produces pressure sores more slowly than any other. 'Sitting on the same spot all day and every day you're bound to get sores, you just can't help it. You get used to it, but you have to work hard to keep them down, because if one gets out of hand, you're in big trouble. There's a spray you use to help them heal, and we use it in conjunction with a very fine talcum powder, and that seems to work quite well. Surprisingly enough, the only really bad sores I've had have been when I was in hospital.' There is only one officially recommended treatment for sores and that is not to subject them to any pressure until they are healed: for most paraplegics that would mean lying face down all day, which is not a popular move.

Wheelchair races can be very exciting events. Until 1976, the International Games featured only straight dashes of 40, 60 and 100 metres (and corresponding relays), but then in Toronto there were full circuit races up to 1500 metres. They tend to fall into a predictable pattern: there is a heck of a scramble to lead round the first bend, and once they can break lanes it becomes a bit of a procession, with the competitors riding in each other's slipstream. As with able-bodied runners, the excitement returns when someone feels he can make a break for the finish - particularly when he is overhauled in the final seconds. The short sprints, in straight lanes, can produce speeds that are quite spectacular. Twenty miles an hour is not uncommon, so it is not surprising that the official rules require the finishing tape to be a length of two-ply white Botany worsted wool. In view of the absence of brakes on racing chairs, spectators are not encouraged to stand beyond the finish line.

The sprint relays are great fun. They take place on a straight track, with scratch lines (for start and finish) drawn across the track at least ten metres in from each end of the track. Each team uses two lanes, the first and third racers racing in one lane, the second and fourth in the other lane, and starting from the other end. The entire chair has to have crossed the scratch line into the takeover zone before the next racer can leave it, and then only when he has been touched on his arm by the incoming man. Those who judge a takeover to perfection use the 10-metre zone to build up speed so that they are touched just as they are about to reach the scratch line.

Perhaps the most entertaining and certainly the most fascinating of wheelchair races is the slalom, which tests not so much power to propel at speed (though the course does end with a straight sprint) as the skill and dexterity with which the man has learned to manipulate his chair. The best of the performers are truly breathtaking in the speed and precision with which they can gyrate through 'gates' (traffic cones) only fractionally wider than the chairs themselves. The distance round the Stoke Mandeville course is about 130 metres. It consists of four approximately equal legs, the first three of which are packed with obstacles.

In a typical course, the slalom racer meets three gates set across his path in the first leg, the second of which he has to go through backwards. At the end of the leg he goes through another gate, round the corner flag, through a gate and round the flag at the start of the second leg. After a short sprint, that brings him to four gates set end on, one after the other, which have to be taken alternately forwards and backwards in a serpentine course. Immediately after that, ramps take him up to and down from a small platform on which he has to spin completely round.

From the ramp he runs down to the flag at the start of the third leg, round that, through one gate backwards and the next forwards, up one step on to a low platform, off it and through another four gates, alternately backwards and forwards. At the end of that leg there is a hairy sequence in which, in the space of only six metres, he must go through a gate, round a flag, through a gate, under a bridge only one metre high, tightly round a flag and sprint 24 metres to the finish. It's a riot.

For sheer excitement, there is nothing in the paraplegic sports programme to touch basketball. To see two high-class teams in opposition is almost sure to be a finer spectacle than to see the game played by able-bodied men without wheelchairs. The skill with which, one-handed, they pass and receive the ball while propelling the chair at speed is quite remarkable ('They have hands like an Arab's feet,' a referee said). The chairs hurtle from one end of the court to the other, twisting and turning, blocking and intercepting. Dribbling is achieved either by propelling the chair with one hand while bouncing the ball with the other; or by bouncing and chair-pushing alternately (two bounces, then two pushes with the ball on the lap). Referees are just as hard on the players as they are in an able-bodied game, and they need to be. There is no lack of determination, aggression and occasionally gamesmanship: one referee, hearing a hiss of air behind him, found that a player had let down one of the tyres of the opposition!

There are some strict regulations applying to chairs in basketball, the most important of which is that there must be a footplate and it must be exactly eleven centimetres from the ground. This, in effect, provides every chair with a bumper: if they hit each other, that is where they hit. If footplates were to vary in height, a collision could result in one footplate crashing into the ankles of another player. Players whose legs are too short for them to reach a footplate eleven centimetres from the ground are not left stranded: they can use blocks, as long as they do not project beyond the front of the footplate.

There are rules to prevent any unfair height advantage being gained, by restricting the height of the seat to fifty-three centimetres (21 in), and stipulating that any cushion used must be no thicker than ten centimetres, and pliable enough to enable both ends to meet when folded. There are no rules against players with long arms, but there is a system that ensures that the average physical capacity of each team is roughly the same, by allocating points to each of the competitive classifications and setting a total points limit on any team.

The only other sport requiring any wheelchair mobility in play is table tennis, and the speed of that game is such that very little ground can be covered. This was one of the very earliest sports introduced by Sir Ludwig into his rehabilitation programme, and it is today one of the most popular paraplegic sports across the world. It is simple and comparatively inexpensive to play, is an ideal recreational pastime to combat the boredom of months in hospital, can often be continued at home and is immediately helpful to both the mind and the body of the patient. The constantly changing pattern of play, with its ceaseless demands for stretching and lunging, provides admirable upper-body exercise and restores the patient's confidence in his ability to balance, a frequent problem following thoracic spinal cord injury. Mentally, even the purely recreational player must keep a sharp mind that is capable of making quick decisions.

Because it is almost impossible for the wheelchair player to reach as far as the net, or to withdraw great distances for the retrieval of a smash, it is unlikely that a paraplegic could ever reach the highest levels of the able-bodied game; but the degree of excellence shown by the best players in the International Games is far beyond that of which most of us with two good legs are capable. One of their major problems is the need either to use one hand to manœuvre the chair during the game, or simply to hang on to the chair for stability. Some grasp the arm of the chair with the free hand, but tetraplegics can often be seen with the free arm hooked round the pushing handle behind the chair to prevent themselves falling forward.

Though the normal rules of the game are as strictly adhered to in table tennis as they are in any other sport the disabled play, one or two concessions are allowed to tetraplegics. As they are likely to suffer from paralysis of the finger and thumb muscles, they may have the bat fastened to their hand, in the normal grip, by a bandage. Because they can't serve from a flat hand, they are allowed to hold the ball between the top of the thumb and forefinger and throw it up to serve. When you realise the small amount of their bodies that retain muscle power (only the deltoid, biceps and triceps need to function in wheelchair table tennis), the level of skill to which an average tetraplegic can train himself is little short of miraculous. Even more extraordinarily, Sir Ludwig once saw a young Norwegian with complete paralysis of all the muscles of both arms who learned to play table tennis with the bat in his mouth. He was even able to serve, when the ball was placed on the bat, and in the International Games of 1962 he beat another tetraplegic of Class 1b: 'It was,' Sir Ludwig wrote, 'one of the most excessive forms of readjustment potentialities in the neuromuscular system I have ever seen.'

Archery will always retain a special place in the history of paraplegic sport, for this was its absolute competitive beginning, and an ideal one. As Sir Ludwig pointed out in his *Textbook of Sport for the Disabled*, its therapeutic value is profound for paraplegics with middle and higher thoracic, and even cervical, lesions, because it develops the muscles of the arms and those muscles of the trunk and shoulder that guarantee the upright position of the patient; it helps the breathing of high-lesion patients; the amount of exercise taken can be increased by shooting greater distances; it is mentally absorbing and stimulating; and it is one of the few sports in which the disabled can, with practice, compete on equal terms with the able-bodied.

Even tetraplegics with finger paralysis can take part, as long as their wrist extensors (stretching muscles) are in good shape. Like the table tennis players, they can be fitted with a special glove to hold the forward hand to the bow, while that which draws the bow string has a slightly curved metal hook built into its glove. Those with one good arm and one that is completely paralysed (or amputated) have a gadget strapped to the chest into which the bow string is caught. It is released by a cable running to a trigger at the bow grip.

All that Sir Ludwig hoped for from his wheelchair archers came to glorious fruition in 1982, when a New Zealand paraplegic, Miss Neroli Fairhall, won the Commonwealth Games gold medal - the able-bodied kind - in Brisbane. She did not take up the sport until she was thirty years old, after a motor cycle crash. In a blustery wind on the last end of the competition, she achieved a most unlikely success by pulling back a five-point deficit with her last three arrows. She finished level on 2,373 points with Janet Yates, of Northern Ireland, and took the gold by virtue of having more hits on target. In such windy conditions was it an advantage, she was asked, to fire from a chair? 'I don't know,' Miss Fairhall replied, 'I've never shot standing up.' That score for a full international FITA round, incidentally, left well behind the International Stoke Mandeville Games record of 2,239 set in Israel by a South African archer, Mrs Margaret Harriman, which had stood since 1968.

Archery is not explosive enough for the fidgety Mrs Price, who couldn't be doing with 'sitting there all day letting off a few arrows'. In any case, she found a particular physical problem when she tried that sport: some damage to the muscles of one eye, sustained in her accident, left it focussing slightly higher than the other and she couldn't use the sight on the bow. She turned to the prime field events of discus, javelin and shot, about which much has already appeared in this book; but there are two peripheral field events for paraplegics and tetraplegics that have not yet been mentioned. Stoke Mandeville used to recognise a distance javelin (the normal kind) and a precision javelin event, which was some kind of cross between archery and darts, and was a competitive exercise favoured by those who could not achieve the powerful thrust needed to hurl the javelin long distances.

A target of eight concentric rings was painted on the grass, about three metres in diameter overall. Men threw the javelin from ten metres and women from seven metres, measured from the centre of the target, and scoring ranged from sixteen points for a bull to two points for the outermost ring. This event no longer figures in competitions.

For competitive classes 1a and 1b, javelin throwing can be replaced by club throwing. The implements are of the Indian club type, bottle-shaped blocks of wood about fifteen inches long and weighing about fourteen ounces. There is a knob at the narrow end, which for those who cannot grip the neck of the 'bottle' normally, can be fitted between the knuckles of their middle two fingers. The club is then hurled from behind the head, to distances of some thirty metres by men and fifteen metres by women. Club throwing is seen more often outside Britain than within it.

In all field events, the throwing must take place within a circle or behind a line, as it does in able-bodied sport. In major competitions there are now usually adjustable anchors to hold the wheelchair rigid from several points on the ground, but where these are not available bodies like Frank Price still snuggle in and hang on. Restraining straps round the competitor's legs are only allowed if the medical identity card shows he is registered for spasm, an uncontrollable reflex action that sometimes occurs in paralysed muscles. This ruling is not popular with those competitors who have particularly long legs: they reasonably claim that extreme effort from their upper half is liable to result in the purely involuntary reflex of their feet kicking off the foot-rest – which makes the throw illegal. In an international competition in Edinburgh some years ago, some of the Australian field events competitors came out to throw with straps holding their chests to the chair backs. They claimed it was legal, but protests by other teams were upheld on the grounds of Stoke Mandeville's general rule for all field events that 'Competitors are forbidden to use any additions or implements fixed to the chair to give them an unfair advantage.' It was interesting to note that when the Australians were forced to throw again without their straps, it made no difference at all to their performance.

At the same time that he introduced archery and table tennis to his paraplegic patients forty years ago, Sir Ludwig had them at skittles. This soon spread, in the post-war years, to ten-pin bowling, but the popularity of both was greatly exceeded by that of the good old-fashioned English game of bowls, at which some wheelchair competitors have proved superb, well up to able-bodied standard at most levels. When the outdoor bowling green was built at Stoke Mandeville, it was adapted for wheelchair use by the addition of concrete zones on which the chairs stood, right up to the edge of the grass, but not on it. Later, the Lady Guttmann Indoor Bowling Centre made life much easier. All the paraplegics needed was a removable ramp at each end to get down to the rink, and a mat from which to bowl. In all other respects the game is exactly the same in or out of wheelchairs, and it is now very widely played across the world.

Snooker is obviously not a difficult game for the wheelchair participant to adapt to, though he finds himself using a rest rather more often than his able-bodied opponent, but one of the surprises at the International Games is the attraction of fencing. A simple floor frame, to which the chairs are clamped, ensures that the chairs are parallel with each other and apart by the distance that, taking into account the length of the weapon and the length of the arms of the fencers involved, allows them to register hits. The close quarters at which these fencers must always fight places on them a strain that can be alleviated by the able-bodied, who are able to retire out of range for a moment's respite. Defence can only be conducted by the hand and the arm; fortunately these are frequently very strong in a paraplegic with a mid-to-low level thoracic injury.

Pupils learning to fence only after they have become disabled need considerable discipline and perseverance. It is a time-consuming sport even for the able-bodied, but its dynamism and elegance make it exciting and very rewarding for the competitor. Female paraplegics do not compete with the épée or sabre, but only with the foil, the lightest of the weapons.

Nor do females compete in weight-lifting, though they often train with weights. Only one kind of lift is recognised by the Stoke Mandeville Games Committee: what they call the Press-on-Bench and most people know as the bench press. The competitor lies supine on a bench, with the weights on their bar supported on an adjustable stand in such a way that the underside of the bar is exactly one inch above the lifter's chest. With a continuous motion, he must lift the bar until it is under control at arms' length; then, still under control, he must lower it to the stand. During the lift his shoulders, buttocks and legs must remain in contact with the bench. Competitors who suffer from severe leg spasms may have their legs strapped to the bench.

In all other respects, the general rules of weight-lifting apply. It goes almost without saying that before any paraplegic is allowed to take up weight-lifting, he is most thoroughly examined by a doctor for any heart or lung deficiency. The sport is in any case only suitable for paraplegics with spinal cord injury no higher than the lumbar region who have retained the function of their abdominal and lower back muscles.

And so to swimming, which for some reason seems to strike the outsider as the most surprising sporting success of them all, though it is in fact one of the most natural. At last the disabled person can leave behind the mechanical reminders of his injury, chairs and calipers and crutches, and be alone in a completely natural environment. Swimming in the form of hydrotherapy is certainly one of the first rehabilitative exercises to which those with spinal cord injuries are directed, and long before Stoke Mandeville had its beautiful 25-metre competitive pool, Sir Ludwig had managed to get installed a 10-metre therapeutic pool at the hospital. It is equipped with an electric hoist that will lower a stretcher into the water and another one that will transfer a patient from a wheelchair into the pool – where the temperature is always between 82 and 85 degrees Fahrenheit (28–30° Centigrade).

A relaxed human body floats naturally in water, and the

only oddity about a floating paraplegic is that the completely paralysed parts of his body float at an angle that varies between 45 degrees for high-cord lesions and 20 degrees for low-cord lesions. Anyone who could swim well before paraplegia will soon swim well with it, and Sir Ludwig used to tell the story of a former patient who fell from a high rock into the sea, hitting another rock during the fall and breaking his spine. He adjusted so quickly to his new condition that he saved his own life by swimming ashore using his arms only. So did the naval officer during the war who, having been thrown into the water when his ship was torpedoed, was then turned into a paraplegic by being hit by a shell. He survived.

Patients who were not experienced swimmers are taught first to swim on their back, 'sculling' by the relaxed movement of their forearms towards the hips. From there they progress to a full overhead backstroke, and are able to see that as each stroke drives them through the water, the paralysed legs that were dangling down at an angle rise almost to the surface. The breaststroke brings particular problems: the body tends to assume an almost upright angle unless it is moving at some speed; and when it is, the buoyancy of the hips tends to cause the head and shoulders to drop, causing the novice to swim with his face in the water. In the freestyle (crawl) stroke, the swimmer has to try to counteract the tendency of his whole trunk and pelvis to rotate. The same tendency exists with the able-bodied, but they can correct it with leg action.

The main difference that is obvious in competition swimming by paraplegics and by the able-bodied is the absence of diving starts. Swimmers are lowered into the water and all races are started with competitors holding on to the end of the bath with at least one hand. For all front strokes, they are allowed one stroke to attain the correct position in the water.

Astounding though the achievements are of disabled

sportsmen in track and field events, of paralysed weight-lifters, of almost immobile table tennis players, there is often, even to the most admiring able-bodied spectator, an element of freakishness about their efforts: of course it is terrific that in Norway there is a lady with a T5 spinal cord injury who has thrown the javelin 14.5 metres, it's amazing. But we all know that a 'normal' accomplished javelin thrower will reach four times that distance. Transfer the ignorant voyeur to the poolside, and the reaction is of a different nature: there he can see that the bodies in the water are deficient. They have, as Margaret put it, 'rag doll' bottom halves - and yet they can perform a function at which the spectator thought he was reasonably adept, and perform it much more efficiently than he can. He can swim, of course he can swim; but he knows that if he got in the water beside Margaret Price, she could give him ten metres start in a 50 metres freestyle race and easily overtake him. That is very impressive. That is no disabled athlete, that is an athlete who happens to be disabled.

13 What Handicap?

It may not take long to get used to the idea of athletes in wheelchairs competing in a wide range of events, but it is more difficult to accept that the blind can race too, and high jump; that the cerebral palsied swim and play basketball; and that there is hardly an athletic event a one-legged man will not master if he wants to. Even in the nineteenth century there were various instances of the involvement of physically handicapped people in sporting events and through the twentieth century occasional individual examples stand out. Douglas Bader, a double leg amputee, will not be forgotten on the golf course; and followers of equestrian sport may remember Denmark's Lis Hartel, who won the dressage silver medal in the Helsinki Olympics of 1952, despite paralysis of her legs caused by poliomyelitis. At the same Games, and also in the previous Games of 1948, gold medals in pistol shooting were won by a Hungarian, Karoly Tacaczs, who had to learn to shoot with his left arm when he lost the right in an accident. And a former world record holder in the hammer, Harold Connolly, of the United States, was partly paralysed in the left hand.

Though there was a sports club for the deaf in Berlin in 1888, there is not much evidence of the organisation of disabled sport until after the Second World War – apart from the Disabled Drivers' Motor Club and the British Society of One-Armed Golfers, one of whom got his handicap down to four. After the war, which left so much disabling injury across the nations of Europe and America, the scene began to change so positively that the British Sports Association for the Disabled was founded in 1961, with headquarters at the Stoke Mandeville Sports Stadium that are provided rent-free by the British Paraplegic Sports Society. It now has four full-time officers and apart from its work of encouraging participation throughout the regions, it organises an annual festival of sport at Stoke Mandeville for many types of disablement - the blind, amputees, cerebral palsied and those with spina bifida, muscular dystrophy and the milder forms of multiple sclerosis.

The BSAD was a founder member of the International Sports Organisation for the Hetero (Multi)-Disabled, which was formed in 1964 and transferred its headquarters from Paris to Stoke Mandeville in 1967. The first World Multi-Disabled Games were held there in 1974, with 212 competitors from twenty-six nations. The next step forward came in 1976, when what used to be known as the Paralympics, or the Wheelchair Olympics, combined in Toronto with the World Games for the blind and amputees. There was a total of 1,560 competitors, including nearly 1,100 paraplegics. Arnhem's Olympics for the Disabled took in the cerebral palsied as well, but by then there had been an objection - a hideously insensitive and inhumane objection - to the use of the word 'Olympic'. It came from the International Olympic Committee, whose Director-General, Monique Berlioux, was presumably only carrying out their wishes when she wrote to Sir Ludwig Guttmann pointing out that nobody has the right to use that word except the IOC themselves - a particularly unfortunate piece of bureaucratic jealousy, since it followed the warm gesture of the IOC in 1976 in agreeing to give its patronage to the Stoke Mandeville Games. For the Games of 1984, in the United States, there was to be a division of activity and another change of title: the VIIth World Wheelchair Games were to take place in the University of Illinois, Champaign, and the Games for the (other) Disabled in Nassau County, New York State.

It is more than a hundred years since two amputees, each equipped with a wooden leg, competed against each other in a walking race on Newmarket Heath, and both the activities and the legs are more sophisticated now. A false limb is known in the business as a prosthesis (an addition), and once the medical designers had got over the crudities supplied immediately after the war, and the deplorable failure to train the amputee properly had been mended, some marvellous work began to be done. For swimming and their athletic events, arm amputees usually discard the prosthesis, and so do single-leg amputees competing in jumping events - perhaps the most extraordinary sight in any disabled sports meeting. Not much less surprising are the extremely agile games of basketball and volleyball played on artificial legs, and you may remember the phenomenal limbless table tennis players at Arnhem.

It was there too that we met the legless Polish woman who won a gold medal by running round the 400-metre track in seven minutes, thanks to artificial limbs, but it is in areas of that kind that one sees public interest in disabled sport going down the drain. To compete is to win, they say, but however much you admire that woman's courage and determination, to stage it as a public spectacle is a mistake. 'That's when disabled sport becomes pathetic,' said Margaret Price. 'I don't see how running alone can be worth a gold medal. If there are two people in a race, you're competing against yourself and the other person and the clock. With one alone there is no competition at all: better to enter a stronger class.'

The matter of classifying amputees originally produced twenty-seven categories for sport, an unwieldy mess that occupied far too much time and frequently resulted in insufficient entrants in each class to provide satisfactory competition. For the 1976 Games in Toronto the categories were reduced to twelve, bringing into one class, for instance, those with a double amputation below the elbow and those with one amputation below and one above the elbow. It is much more difficult than you might expect to learn to run without your full complement of arms. For a start, the body is unbalanced, and this can be compounded by the fact that the shoulder muscles over an amputated arm still tend to work as hard as if it were there. Without the original weight to contend with, the muscles can become grossly distorted. Furthermore, a high-arm amputation - and particularly a double - produces a considerable impairment in the ventilatory capacity of the lungs, making the speedy intake of breath during running more difficult.

Limbless swimmers with an arm amputation on one side have the particular problem of trying to keep in a straight line. Without compensation, the natural course is either a diagonal or a complete circle! It is amazing to see how, with practice, even double-arm amputees can swim both breaststroke and backstroke adequately, using not just their stumps and their legs, but compensatory muscular mechanisms of the trunk to propel them through the water. Turning at the end of the pool when you are swimming on your back without arms is a problem that it takes some time to overcome; but, with persistence, the swimmer seems to sense the moment to turn, fish-like, and touch the end with his feet.

In terms of classifying patients to produce 'fair play' in sports competition, no area is more difficult to judge than that of cerebral palsy. Its sufferers, all loosely and incorrectly called 'spastics' by the general public, show such widely-differing degrees of physical or mental disability that the sports organiser - who is not greatly helped by the official medical assessment - can only do his best to sort them out. Discontent and frustration is the frequent result of inaccurate classification in this extremely complex group of afflictions, but Dr Guttmann's philosophy was that the physical training of cerebral palsy victims from a very early age makes them aware of the relationship of one part of the body to the others, and can thus lead to the control of unwanted reflex movements. Track events, ball games, archery and particularly swimming have proved popular with the cerebral palsied.

Because of their great need for compensation, the blind develop an extraordinary sense of touch, hearing and awareness denied to the fully-sighted, and it is deeply rewarding as well as very exciting to see them mastering athletic events that the rest of us could hardly believe they would attempt. If anybody doubts the value of their involvement in sport, they should have heard Bill Griffiths' address to the first conference of the BSAD at Stoke Mandeville in 1973. Griffiths, a prisoner-of-war in a Japanese camp, was blinded and lost both forearms in the war:

> 'Many people want to know why we disabled persons, and particularly blind people, trouble ourselves with competitive sports. We can't hope to achieve the same results as able-bodied people - little likelihood of ever becoming a success, in the eyes of sports journalists anyway, but when we think about it, that word "success" is a very irrelevant term. It may well mean the top-class athlete running the mile in something under four minutes, but it can equally mean a disabled person just completing one length of the swimming bath.
>
> Great satisfaction can be had in just learning a new sport under professional care, thereby discovering some way of lessening or maybe eliminating one's own physical disadvantage. It's good to improve on a previous performance. At a sports meeting, I've been very dissatisfied with my performance and that's been an incentive

and challenge to do better next time, and I've practised for weeks to knock the odd inch off to do better; and when the sports have come round here it's been good to pip a colleague to the post who normally pips me to it.

Physically, sports loosen up the joints and keep the muscles strong, help us blind persons to balance much better. It enables our stout-hearted, resilient friends in wheelchairs to keep the upper halves of their anatomy in good shape. It brings about this physical feeling of well-being, and it can eradicate many nervous disorders too.

I've got one friend at St Dunstan's who ten years ago was completely confined to a wheelchair. And how he has deserted that chair! Four years ago he did, in fact, complete a 1½-mile walking race. Two years ago he married one of the pretty girls he met at the sports meetings. Sports have done him a world of good.

Psychologically, it can have a profound effect. It can help us to banish many fears and frustrations.'

Some sports for the blind can only be accomplished with the help of acoustic signalling devices. Sprinters run one at a time against the clock on a straight 60-metre or 100-metre track. They start on the centre line, which on a six-lane track is the line separating lanes three and four. Hopefully, the blind runner will stay on or about this line, which to him is known as lane five. The lane to his right is three and that to his left is four. His coach, at the finish line, calls incessantly to him: 'Five, five, five ...' if he is running straight; 'Three, three ...' if he needs to move to the right; and 'Four, four ...' if he needs to go left. Aiming at the voice, the experienced sprinter keeps uncannily straight and plenty fast: the 34-year-old Scottish runner Willy McLeod won the 60 metres in Arnhem in 7.70 seconds. For longer races, on the circuit, blind runners and walkers are escorted by sighted and athletic companions, loosely attached to them by lines at the waist or the wrist. The escort must keep slightly behind his man and to one side, and thus keeps him on his course.

To see them attack the high jump is an unbelievable experience: the competitor stands at the bar, feels its height and then moves backwards – either a pace, for a standing jump, or a full running distance. In the latter case, the coach stays at the bar, giving a vocal signal. Into the blackness runs the competitor, often judging the take-off to perfection. Not much less amazing are the blind bowlers, some of whom achieve superb accuracy just by being talked to the jack by a sighted companion: 'You're at four o'clock, John, and three feet out.' An even more surprising skill in finding a target is that now being shown by some blind archers. Though the sport has not yet spread widely enough to be accepted on the international programme, astonishing progress has been made at St Dunstan's Institute for the Blind, near Brighton.

Two members of the staff there passed the Grand National Archery Society's coaching examinations, and one of them was blind. (Officially registered as 'partially sighted', his range of vision at the time was no more than three metres). They formed what may have been the world's first properly constituted blind archery club at the Institute, the residents of which are all war-blinded, and some of them have since joined able-bodied clubs. The critical difference between blind archers and sighted ones is obviously that the 'sight' they use must be a tactile and not a visual one, and at St Dunstan's they devised an adjustable pointer mounted on a tripod which the archer feels with the knuckles of his leading hand. Additionally, fixed markers on the ground ensure that the feet are in the right position, and the presence of the coaches helps to line up the shoulders correctly and to 'read' the result on the target.

One of the happiest sights in disabled sport is the face of a novice blind archer when he hears his arrow hit the target for the first time, and they soon learn to listen for the difference in the sound of the arrow as it strikes closer to the centre of the target. They begin on an indoor, twenty-yard range, and the proficient archers move outside in the summer to ranges of up to forty yards. The blind coach there has even achieved some success at sixty yards without using his tripod sight.

For many of the St Dunstan's patients, blindness is not the only problem. Some are in wheelchairs (which, as we have seen, is no great handicap to an archer); some are arm amputees, and even that does not stop them taking up archery. Prostheses can be fitted with all manner of little tools to cope with problems like that, and one archery coach happily faced the problem of making it possible for a (sighted) thalidomide youngster to handle a bow, though her right hand was attached to her shoulder and her left arm was about half the normal length. It's impossible! No, Sir Ludwig would not allow that word to be used, and nor do many others in the disabled game: a combination of an extension from the bow to the left hand, and a leather mouth-tab with which the bow string could be drawn back, allowed the young lady to make a start. Give the disabled half a chance and they're away. The blind are not particularly well served with recreational facilities, but when the Rotary Clubs of Britain organised a blind sports day at Stoke Mandeville in 1982 there were nearly 400 competitors, and even judo was on the programme.

Perhaps, as Margaret Price said, it is time we stopped gawping at what the handicapped regard as perfectly normal behaviour, and began to enjoy it as much as they do. Water skiing, you might think, is out of the question for amputees: never. The British Disabled Water Ski Association is full of one-legged and one-armed enthusiasts and even boasts some blind members who have skied across the Channel. Its chairman, Tony Edge, devised first the 'Heron Strut' to give extra support to the one-legged, and then the brilliant 'Edge Triple Bar'. This comprises three metal handles with independent ropes to the towing boat, which telescope together to form one wide tow bar. The nervous novice skis in the middle with an instructor on either side. As he becomes more stable, the handle can be slid apart, leaving him to ski solo with assistance near at hand. For the one-armed there is the marvellous 'Delgar Sling', which is attached at one end to a cup on the end of a ski handle and at the other to a body harness, and yet is instantly released when the skier's able hand lets go.

Paraplegics, of course, will have to sit this one out? Only if they want to. When members of the BDWSA attended a competition in Belgium, they discovered the 'Sitz Ski', a kind of a small sledge designed for those who cannot stand and ski. It was in use in September 1983, during the first British Open disabled water ski championships, held at the Heron Lake Centre, a disused gravel pit in Berkshire presented to the Association by Hall Aggregates. It is only the ignorance of the rest of us that causes our astonishment: the blind and amputees have been snow skiing for years internationally, and in the 1980 winter 'Olympics' for the disabled, in Norway, paraplegics joined in too – on a 'Polk', a free-running sled steered by the use of short ski sticks.

Awareness is slowly growing in Britain of the joy that can be brought to the handicapped through sport, and often particularly through competitive sport. In the past two or three years there have been held the Special Olympics for the mentally handicapped (what did the IOC think of that one?), the British Transplant Games (there were Transplant Olympics in Athens in 1982), the World Games for the Deaf and the National Games for *Les Autres* (the others), held to give sporting opportunity to those whose disabilities do not fall within other organised groups – people suffering from arthritis and rheumatism, for example, or from conditions caused by injuries that partially destroyed nerves, joints and muscles. Sports meetings of the handicapped are never likely to fill Wembley Stadium - though it is interesting to note that 100,000 people visited the Wheelchair Olympics in Tokyo in 1964, and that there were 25,000 at the opening ceremony of the Games in Israel four years later - but at least they indicate progress not only by the disabled, but by society at large towards the disabled.

As Sir Ludwig pointed out, despite the fact that two world wars produced millions of disabled, it is only in recent years that the community has begun to take a positive approach to the severely disabled, and to accept them as a part of itself. What society now seems to need more than anything is the recognition that the physically disabled do not want sympathy as much as they want empathy - the ability to project one's own personality into another's and thus acquire true understanding of his problems.

Sport for the disabled is not only the most natural form of remedial exercise, it helps to restore what Guttmann called 'that passion for playful activity and the desire to experience joy and pleasure in life, so deeply inherent in any human being.' Finally, and perhaps supremely, sport for the disabled person helps to restore his contact with the world around him - often the very greatest of all his losses.

However determined those disabled sportsmen are to win, it does seem that they fill the holes in their lives with a mixture not commonly seen in the able-bodied. In the basketball hall, you may well find an expert Israeli giving help and encouragement to the suffering Egyptian team. With such an international gesture these sportsmen set the world an example, and it sits sweetly at Stoke Mandeville amid the whooping and the hollering, the sunbathing and the snogging - don't think this lot are not interested in the temptations of the flesh - the racing and the rejoicing.

They are dedicated athletes no less remarkable in their prowess than the wondrous performers we see in the able-bodied arenas of the world; but they have something else. The foul stroke of fortune that struck them down left them with a compensatory back-hander, a blessing the size of which is hard to encompass and the source of which is likely to remain a mystery to most of us. The certainty of its existence is confirmed when you hear the words of an American athlete, Ray Clark, a polio victim with seventy-five international gold medals: 'If I had to live my life all over again, I'd hardly change a thing. I'd want to be handicapped just the same.'

14 Doors Shut, Doors Open

As if 1981 had not already provided its share of drama, an event of bizarre and theatrical tragedy awaited the Prices one night in August. Margaret had opened a fête in Chagford, a little Devon town on Dartmoor, and stayed to present the prizes in the evening. Friends from Stoke Mandeville had been staying with them, and when all was done in Chagford the two families piled in the van for the long journey back to Buckinghamshire.

It was late, and dark, when they reached the village of Stone, a few miles west of Aylesbury. Both Frank and Margaret, in the front of the van, saw in the headlights the figure of a woman in white on the roadside to their right. 'She put a cigarette to her lips and had that last draw,' recalled Margaret, 'then she stepped out. I shall never forget it.' As the woman ran to the middle of the road, Frank's instinct took him away from her, to the left. In his carriageway she stopped and faced his lights, her eyes shut, her hands clenched into her long dressing gown, her feet bare.

If Frank had braked hard then, he would have hit her full on, smash; but he never braked hard, because of the danger to Margaret's neck. Now there was more room to the right. He hauled on the wheel and hurled the van past her. In terrible frustration, she dived for the van and just missed it. On the right-hand pavement Frank brought the van to a halt and they sat there, sick and shaking. One of their passengers went to phone the police. Behind them, another car had stopped.

To what dreadful degree of despair had that poor woman been driven? What rage, what pain, what fear had sent her so frantically to seek her death? What gruesome chance had decreed that she should do so at the feet of Margaret Price, who just eight years earlier had crossed a road in joy, never to cross one on her legs again?

Within a month Margaret was back in hospital. It is not easy for a paraplegic to pinpoint just why, or even where, she does not feel well, and it is a lot harder for the doctor. Unable to find anything positively wrong with her, he presumed she had picked up an infection of some sort and prescribed antibiotics: 'Come back and see me again if they don't do the trick.' They didn't. Her headaches - not ever-present, but a permanent threat in her life ever since the accident - became more frequent and more painful. She was admitted to hospital in Barnstaple, about forty miles from her home, on the north Devon coast, and a form of spinal meningitis was diagnosed.

Two generations ago, meningitis was invariably fatal, but those times have passed - though tuberculous meningitis, if not swiftly arrested, can still be a most dangerous disease. It arises from a bacterial infection that causes inflammation of the membranes covering either the brain (cerebral meningitis) or the spinal cord. In Margaret's case the infection was of comparatively low intensity, but it attacked the weak spot in her neck - the area of the third cervical nerve, where there had been minor damage when her spine was broken lower down. When she left hospital a fortnight later she was wearing a surgical collar, and still does; her left hand (the weak one) was noticeably weaker and the good right hand, that had thrown so many implements far across so many sports fields, was no longer the force that it used to be. Picking up her beaker of coffee (paraplegics drink absolutely gallons of anything, to keep the bladder flushed) was now a two-handed job and the fingers were a lot less flexible than they were.

'When I came out of hospital my doctor used to call quite a bit, and one day he came in looking a bit uncomfortable. I said, "D'you want a coffee?" and he said "Yes please." I went into the kitchen to get it and I called out to him, "I know what you're going to say." "You do?" he said, really surprised. "Yes," I said, "what you're going to say is, it's time to pack up sport. I've already accepted that." You should have seen the look of relief on his face.

'When I was in Barnstaple I think I knew the time had come. I love sport and I love competing, but I knew I had to call it a day. If you're honest with yourself, you know what your body has taken and you know what your body is capable of doing. No matter how much you want to go on, you're the one who really knows when the time has come to say, that's it. I could have gone on, yes. It wouldn't have been the same, but I'm not helpless. I could have gone on, in a different class, but I didn't know what I might be doing to my body if I did.'

It was a shock to see Margaret that winter, so much less active than she had been, looking rather more like a disabled person ought to look! But if her body had taken a beating, there still wasn't a lot they could do to quench her spirit. By the Spring, she was raring to go again - down another road: 'It's not the end for me, this, you know. Okay, so one door has shut in my face; but I would have had to give up competing at some time anyway. I don't reckon it's a door shutting at all, really, it's another door opening, a new opportunity. All the time I was competing, I couldn't do half the things I wanted to do, because there wasn't time, I was always training. Now I can do the other half: I can coach disabled children and try to promote sport for the disabled and hopefully do some good all along the line.

'A lot of people are saying to me now, "Don't you miss

sport?" And I don't, because we're doing so much else now. I've got so much to look forward to and to live for now, other things, new things, and just the excitement of competing wouldn't be enough to exchange for all the rest of it. I never wanted to be a has-been anyway, and that's what would have happened. It's sad to see people like that, people who have stayed in sport so long they're nothing like as good as they used to be. I only competed for a few years, I know, but those years were fantastic, weren't they?'

You could say that, Mrs Price, you could say that: in four summers, twenty gold medals at the International Games; in five summers, seventeen world records set in five different events. An MBE, two disabled sports personality of the year awards, two sports personality of the week awards, *This Is Your Life* – a good deal more than most of us achieve in a lifetime. Then she drew breath, gave Frank a gee-up, and they shot off down the next road.

'Frank was ever so shy and quiet before we married, and he used to worry. Beads of sweat used to come on his forehead. I'd say, "Stop worrying, Frank, it's a waste of energy. We can use that energy." We've really been good for each other. We used to go off to meet people, big occasions like dinners and speaking engagements and that sort of thing, and he'd be definitely worried about the prospect. I used to say, "Don't be nervous, Frank, they're only people," and he'd enjoy it. We met a bloke the other day that Frank used to work with. Hadn't seen him for years, and this fellow says, "Good God, Frank, what have you been up to? You look years younger." Frank was pleased with that. We make a right pair, don't we? With his disability and my disability we'd just about make up one good body between us.'

Margaret, the woman with no more than one-third of a working body, reckons they have been privileged – they had the fun of competing and now they have the fun of trying to help the children. (It's nearly always 'we' when Margaret talks, Frank is not left out: 'Didn't touch our records in the '82 Internationals, did they Frank?') It has either never occurred to her, or she has long since dismissed the idea, that she has had a bloody raw deal from life. How much more can you take and still come up smiling?

'No, it's not like that at all, not a bit. Things happen to everybody, don't they – bit of bad luck here, bit of bad luck there – but you don't let it upset the rest of your life. do you? And whatever's happened to me, I've loved life right from the beginning. My life changed pretty dramatically along the way, as you know, but I honestly couldn't say that I don't enjoy it now because of what happened to me, the accident. It just wouldn't be true, I do enjoy it, I love it. I've done things, had experiences that I never would have had if I'd remained able-bodied, and that's my reward, I suppose. People think it must be boring, stuck in a wheelchair all day. But the day goes too quickly, I can't get everything in.'

Down in Devonshire they call this maid of Kent 'our Margaret', and you don't get many warmer compliments than that. She will go anywhere to speak, to talk, to encourage, to exhort, to act as local celebrity. Wherever she goes she spreads the message, by her very presence, that the disabled must not be written off; that apart from the inconvenience of not being able to use his legs, there is nothing peculiar about a paraplegic: 'If I wanted to excel at something I could do sitting down, playing bridge, say, then it wouldn't be "Disabled bridge player Margaret Price". It should be the same with sport. The day you take up sport is the day you leave your disability behind and start looking forward.'

And that is the message she tries to drum into the youngsters they meet in the schools for the disabled – though some of those, like the loos, are more like disabled schools. She and Frank go to the junior games for the disabled and the junior paraplegic games and try to make contacts from the various special schools about the country, and particularly in the west country. They visit as many schools as will invite them, and occasionally one that doesn't, cajoling and urging greater sports provision out of the staff, encouraging and leading the young to attempt the unknown and achieve the impossible. The Prices are incessant adventurers and relentless crusaders, drawing constant joy from the land in which they live and fighting harder than ever to fill the lives of the disabled with good things.

'It doesn't matter what the disability is, I'll coach anyone. Disability is not the common bond, sport is. The disability is soon forgotten when you work on the ability. It's a very taxing job, to work out what movement the children have got and how best they can use it, but it's a very rewarding job when you see the joy of discovery on some little fellow's face.'

Not everything she finds in the schools pleases her, and though most of it is not her business, she can't resist trying to improve the situation. There are some schools for the handicapped, she says, where far from building up the children's ego and morale, they seem to do their best to knock the stuffing out of them. And often the biggest disability some children have is their parents, who either mollycoddle them and talk for them, or fail to accept or recognise their responsibilities towards them. Nevertheless, as the months of her mission tick by, so she builds her flock of talent. One day, she says, there will be a Margaret Price sports team for the disabled and they will challenge the British team and beat them – and though there is that wicked glint in her eye as she says it, there is a touch of grimness in the undertone that suggests it may not be a joke. She is a critical lady, is Margaret, and she no longer believes, now that 'Poppa' Guttmann has gone, that all is well at Stoke Mandeville. 'Sometimes I say things that could get us in a bit of a mess, and Frank gets us out of it: "Take no notice of her," he says, "she's in a wheelchair."'

In the summer of 1983 she was out of her wheelchair for a long time. After suffering growing aggravation with her digestive system through the year, she was admitted to the Royal Naval Hospital at Plymouth, where she stayed for more than two months. It seems likely, they decided, that the original accident did more damage to the autonomic nervous system than was apparent at the time, and some of her internal organs have begun to misbehave. The answer, of course, is pills and pills and pills, and at least they work some of the time. Her stay at Plymouth ('a smashing hospital') was prolonged, wouldn't you know, by a pressure sore formed during x-rays. In their efforts to heal it, the staff took the prescribed action and laid Margaret face down on the bed - a situation from which a paraplegic has no means of escaping. Something was wrong, possibly a pinched nerve in the neck, and when they at last turned her up again she had lost the use of her right arm. It wasn't just a case of 'pins and needles', for though the power slowly trickled back, it still had not reached her thumb several weeks later.

As it was a forty-mile drive from the cottage to Plymouth, and Frank could not contemplate failing to see Margaret every day, he filled the van with his 'smalls', the dog and the budgerigar, and camped out on the moors all summer, a few miles from the hospital. The pressure sore was very slow to respond to treatment, and in the end Frank was allowed to take the lady home provided he continued to nurse her properly. They decided to let nature take a hand in the affair: 'I rigged up a shelter in the garden for her,' said Frank, 'and exposed her little bum to the sun. Did her no end of good. What we had to be careful of then was not getting it burned!'

It has seen some sights, that innocent little patch of Devonshire. The grass roots are ventilated by a thousand javelin points, the roses trimmed by a myriad discus throws. And think of those shots, three-kilo lumps thudding into the ground in all weathers. 'I used to love my training,' Margaret said happily, 'all the time I did it I loved it, right up to the last competition. But it's quite nice to think that now I haven't *got* to go out and do it, I haven't *got* to get up at some ungodly hour to go out in the garden and put the shot. Frank used to reel in the tape sometimes and it was caked in ice. He used to put the shot in the oven to warm it up a bit first, it was so cold it burned my hands. Yes, I loved it, but you can't go on for ever.'

Forty years ago, she would not have gone on at all. Before Guttmann, she would have had no chance to warm her hands before the fire of life, but with what relish she has done so! 'Well, if I can't enjoy what I've got, I might as well give up. But I do enjoy it, all of it, every day. Whatever we do, it's fun.' And what of death, the undiscovered country, is that a shadow that she has let herself recognise?

'It's not something that worries me. I assume that if you spend your life in a chair, nothing but sitting in a chair, you're going to pick up some problems – never mind the ones you had to start with. If you look at it logically, a paraplegic isn't going to hold out as long as an able-bodied person – but then you get exceptions everywhere. You get some able-bodied people living to a terrifically old age, and some dying terribly young. There's not a lot any of us can do about it. You can think about it, of course you can, but all the thinking in the world won't give you the answer. If my life is going to be shorter than that of the girls I went to school with, then I'm going to make the most of it. I know that at the end I shall be able to say I've enjoyed what I've had, and that's one important thing. And the other is, I just want to know that when my time comes,

I've done some things I can be proud of. That's all that really matters. To me.

'There is something that bothers me, though. With that lump of cement in my knee, I don't suppose they'll let me be cremated. It'd bung up the works, wouldn't it? Tell you what, we'll have a coffin made of driftwood, with rope handles and a single flower. That would suit me well - and all the money that's saved can go to carry on the work for disabled children.'

Appendix A

Classification of Paraplegics and Tetraplegics for Competitive Sport

The higher the spinal cord injury, the greater the loss of power and feeling: on this fact, the classification is based, though the medical officers involved are urged by the Executive Committee of the International Stoke Mandeville Games Federation to take account of functional ability as well as pure neurological deficit. A paraplegic with a spinal cord injury low in the thoracic region may have developed a deformity of the spine which gives him the postural problems of a patient with a higher injury; and a competitor with an injury so placed that it should put him in Class 3 may have developed such skill and postural control that it would be fairer to class him lower. The whole object of these classifications is to ensure fair play and as far as possible to eliminate injustices. Sir Ludwig Guttmann himself warned the examining doctors that some competitors might exaggerate their disability during examination in order to be classed as more severely disabled than they really are.

Tetraplegics (those with some degree of paralysis in all four limbs) are sub-divided into three groups, according to the position and severity of the neck injury:

Class 1a injury to the upper cervical spinal cord (at or

below C6) with the triceps muscles not functional against gravity.

Class 1b neck injury below C6/7 with good working of the triceps and the wrist extensor and flexor muscles (extensors straighten, flexors bend), but with no finger flexors or extensors of functional value.

Class 1c neck injury below C8 with good triceps and good flexors and extensors to the long fingers, but without any functional value to those muscles controlled by the first thoracic segment (T1).

(In all tetraplegic classifications the function and strength of the muscles of the shoulder girdle must be taken into account.)

Class 2 injury to the thoracic spinal cord from below T1 to T5 inclusive; having no balance when sitting.

Class 3 injury from below T6 to T10 inclusive; ability to keep balance when sitting.

Class 4 injury below T11 to L3 (lumbar) inclusive, provided there is no function of the major muscles of the thigh and the buttocks.

Class 5 injury below L4, with reasonable thigh and buttock muscle function.

Class 6 spinal injuries with minimal muscular deficit.

(A points system taking account of the function of the muscles of the lower limbs operates for Classes 4, 5 and 6.)

Appendix B

Final Placings Achieved by Margaret Price in the International Stoke Mandeville Games (Class 2)

1978

Swimming:	50m backstroke	1st (*new world record*)
	50m breaststroke	4th
	50m freestyle	1st (*new world record*)
Field events:	Discus	1st
	Javelin	7th
	Shot	2nd

1979

Swimming:	50m backstroke	1st
	50m breaststroke	1st
	50m freestyle	1st
	Individual medley	1st
	Team medley relay	1st
	Team freestyle relay	1st (*new world record*)
Field events:	Discus	1st (*new world record*)
	Shot	1st (*new world record*)

1980 (Arnhem):

Swimming:	50m backstroke	1st
	50m breaststroke	3rd
	50m freestyle	1st
	Individual medley	1st
	Team medley relay	2nd
	Team freestyle relay	1st (*new world record*)

Field events:	Discus	2nd
	Javelin	3rd
	Shot	1st

(In the swimming events, the 50m backstroke and freestyle were new individual world records by virtue of it being the first time they had been swum in a 50m pool rather than in one of 25m.)

1981

Swimming:	50m backstroke	2nd
	50m breaststroke	2nd
	50m freestyle	1st (*new world record*)
	Individual medley	1st
	Team medley relay	1st
	Team freestyle relay	1st
Field events:	Discus	1st (*new world record*)
	Javelin	2nd
	Shot	1st

Appendix C

Paraplegic Class 2 World Records set by Margaret Price

Swimming: 50m backstroke (short course)
1977 – 57.10 sec (previously 63.20)
1978 – 51.50
1980 – 51.40
1981 – 50.78 (subsequently reduced by a Swedish competitor to 45.29)

50m backstroke (long course)
1980 – 51.38 (new event)

50m freestyle (short course)
1977 – 56.60 (previously 62.20)
1978 – 50.60
1979 – 45.70
1981 – 44.91
1981 – 42.72

50m freestyle (long course)
1980 – 45.10 (new event)

3 × 25m individual medley
1980 – 1 min 22.42 sec
1981 – 1 min 21.44 sec

(At the time of her retirement, the 50m breaststroke world record (short course) stood at 59.63 sec. Mrs Price's best time in 1981 was 60.24.)

Field events: Discus

1979 – 15.04 metres (previously 14.99)
1980 – 15.74 (subsequently beaten by a Norwegian competitor with 16.16m)
1981 – 17.42

Shot

1979 – 5.45m (previously 5.28)

(At the time of her retirement, the world javelin record stood at 14.50m. Mrs Price's best throw in 1981 was 10.84.)

Appendix D

National Organisations for Disabled People

British Sports Association for the Disabled, Ludwig Guttmann Sports Centre, Harvey Road, Aylesbury, Bucks. Tel: 0296 27889. (Co-ordinating body for sports activities for all disabled people.)

Scottish Sports Association for the Disabled, 14 Gordon Court, Dalclavehouse, Dundee.

Welsh Sports Association for the Disabled, The Bungalow, South Wales Equitation Centre, Heol-y-Cyw, Bridgend, Mid-Glamorgan.

Association of Spina Bifida & Hydrocephalus, Miss M. Gilbertson, Tavistock House North, Tavistock Square, London WC1.

British Amputee Sports Association, Dr G. Thomas, 110 Speed House, Barbican, London EC2.

British Association for Sporting and Recreational Activities of the Blind, RMIB, Chaucer Street, Nottingham.

British Deaf Sports Council, 1 Sandholme Drive, Burley-in-Wharfedale, West Yorkshire.

British Disabled Water Ski Association, Warren Wood, The Warren, Ashtead, Surrey.

British Epilepsy Association, Crowthorne House, New Wokingham Road, Wokingham, Berkshire.

British Les Autres Association, 239a Thomas Close, Southgate, Runcorn, Cheshire.

British Limbless Ex-Services Association, 185–187 High Road, Chadwell Heath, Essex.
British Paraplegic Sports Society, Ludwig Guttmann Sports Centre, Harvey Road, Aylesbury, Bucks.
British Polio Fellowship, Mr Leo Jackson, Bell Close, West End Road, Ruislip, Middlesex.
British Ski Club for the Disabled, Corton House, Corton, nr. Warminster, Wiltshire.
Muscular Dystrophy Group, Nattrass House, 35 Macaulay Road, London SW4.
National Association of Visually Handicapped Bowlers, Mr J. Hughes, 58 Dudley Close, Leicester.
National Federation of Gateway Clubs, Mr J. Oliver, 117–123 Golden Lane, London EC1.
Opportunities for Disabled, 1 Bank Buildings, Princes Street, London EC2.
Royal National Institute for the Blind, 224–226 Great Portland Street, London W1.
St Dunstan's, 191 Marylebone Road, London NW1.
Shaftesbury Society, Shaftesbury House, 112 Regency Street, London SW1.
Spastics Society, 12 Park Crescent, London W1.
Wheelchair Dance Association, Craig-y-Parc School, Pentyrch, Cardiff.